500
Computing Tips for Teachers and Lecturers

500 Tips from Kogan Page

500

Computing
Tips *for* *Teachers*
and *Lecturers*

PHIL RACE AND STEVE McDOWELL

**KOGAN
PAGE**

To our wives, Liz and Sally

First published in 1996

Kogan Page Limited
120 Pentonville Road
London N1 9JN

British Library Cataloguing in Publication Data

A CIP record for this book is available from the British Library.

ISBN 0 7494 1931 8

Typeset by BookEns Ltd, Royston, Herts.
Printed and bound in Great Britain by Clays Ltd St. Ives PLC

Contents

Preface

The revolution is already with us when it comes to computers and information technology (IT). Everyone's life is being affected in one way or another, whether as users of the new machines or receivers of the products of the new technologies. The number of related books, magazines, journal articles and on-line Web discussions grows daily. A consequence of the information revolution is that the distance between technophobes and technophiles is widening rapidly. Once it was perfectly all right to be a technophobe, and such people could conduct their lives and work without worrying about computers or information technology. This is no longer the case for most people, and the need to launch newcomers gently into the multimedia age is causing many people to venture into the new culture. The problem, when there is one, is usually how to take those first steps. This can seem daunting. We've written this book to ease the journey into the world of keyboards, monitors, disk-drives, mousepads and megabytes.

Gaining competence in using information technology is a process that is best reached through the following approaches:

- an active, learning-by-doing approach, in other words hands-on;
- learning by trial and error;
- hundreds of small learning experiences, one at a time;
- thousands of decision-making episodes, one at a time;
- making best use of other people's existing knowledge and experience.

We have designed this book to accommodate, as well as we can, all of the factors listed above. We have particularly tried to start from scratch in all the important areas, so that readers with no previous knowledge or experience of computers or information technology can get started. We hope to have made this possible without them necessarily having to plough through the thick (and sometimes unfriendly) manuals that come with most hardware or software. We've added a glossary at the end of the book, covering many of the words and phrases which may seem like a foreign language to those entering the field for the first time.

Many readers will not be starting from scratch, but will know some areas well, and others not at all. We intend such readers to head straight for the parts of our book which may help them, and mostly ignore things we've written about the topics they know already. However, we would encourage such readers to at least glance at what we've written about things that may be familiar, as even finding just one useful extra tip on a subject can be worthwhile – we are often surprised ourselves when we find an unexpected tip or wrinkle about something we thought we knew all about.

We don't pretend that we've covered everything. In a field as big as this, we could only try to provide a skeleton coverage of the aspects of computing and information technology that are most central to most people. We hope, however, that our suggestions will be enough to help you on your way, and to develop your confidence so that you will be ready to embark on further adventures in the field.

Five ways of using this book

There's no 'right way' of making the most of a book of this sort, and how you will get the best value from it will depend on you, and the circumstances you're addressing. However, we think it may be useful to alert you to some of the approaches.

1   Decide what you need help on, then use the contents page and index to find where it's mentioned.

2   Scan through the contents and decide where you'd like to start.

3   Use relevant sections as checklists, ticking off items that you've already attended to, putting crosses beside suggestions that aren't relevant to you, and maybe putting question marks beside those that you may wish to think about again.

4   Identify the area you're going to address, find the pages where we've given tips, then talk through our suggestions with someone who knows. This way, you are likely to get extra help quickly if you need it.

5   If you are teaching other people how to use information technology, you may find some of our sets of suggestions useful as 'starting-point agendas' for class discussion, or for helping individual students.

Chapter 1 Getting Started With Computers

This chapter may reach you too late — after you've chosen and purchased your computer! However, we are sure that some of our suggestions will be of value to you, maybe sooner than you think; you may well be updating, upgrading or even replacing your entire system before long. The intensity of the development of hardware and software is such that everything tends to become out-of-date almost as soon as we buy it; more frustratingly, real costs keep coming down. It is upsetting to see an equivalent (or better) system available for less than you paid only a little while ago, and it's hard to feel that any purchase is a real bargain. That said, whether you get good value from your investment in computing depends on two main factors: whether you make full use of what you've bought, and whether it works well for you in the ways that you intended when you bought it.

We start with some suggestions on selecting your computer, and we hope some of these will help save you money at the same time as ensuring that the shelf life of your system is as good as you can make it. We follow this with advice on actually clinching the deal. Next we look at 'cheap or free items' — you may be surprised at how useful some of the software can be that you can get at negligible cost.

Our next sections should be worth looking at whether you're just setting up a new system, or comfortably settled with your old system. In fact, 'comfortably' is an important word, and we'd like to ensure that you give due thought to your own comfort when you use your system, especially if you're likely to be using it for hours at a time. After attending to the comfort dimensions, we move on to safety. Perhaps we should have introduced safety first — but we think you will feel more like making sure that you're safe if you have already attended to your comfort!

Individuals have their own views on environmental issues, so we appreciate that our suggestions on 'green issues' will be regarded as important by some, and as mere detail by others. However, both authors are quite concerned about these issues, so we needed to include these for our own consciences as well as to trigger awareness in our readers.

We end this chapter with a 'panic page', which we hope you will never need to use! We know how upsetting it can be when things go wrong — particularly when 'it was all right yesterday, and now I can't do anything with it'. People who have become dependent on a system can feel as if both arms have been amputated when the system won't work. We aim to help in two ways: firstly to help you get things in proportion when things go wrong, and secondly to help you check out all of the relatively straightforward things before you decide that you really need to panic!

1

Choosing a computer

There is a bewildering range of personal computers to choose from. Choosing the wrong one will lead to difficulties, so spend time investigating the options before choosing.

1   **Decide what you need a computer for.** Be realistic about your needs. If your needs are modest, a modest computer will be satisfactory. If you plan to use the computer for sophisticated work, you will need to make sure you choose a computer that will be up to the task.

2   **Decide on a budget.** There is no obvious upper limit to the amount that could be spent on a computer. You must operate within constraints, so find out what they are. Don't forget that you may have to budget for software, blank disks, printers and other items.

3   **Find out what your colleagues are using.** If you know other computer users, ask them what system they are using and what they think of it. If the system you choose is compatible with theirs (that is, it can use the same software and data), you will be able to seek (and offer) help, and collaborative work will be easier.

4   **Check what support your institution can offer.** If you have access to support from a computing department or information technology centre, find out what kind of systems they are prepared to work with. They could be your main source of help if you have problems. If they regularly purchase computers, they may be able to help you buy one at a good price.

5   **Choose your supplier with care.** Try to buy from a specialist computer supplier who will be able to answer your questions and who will be able to give you an acceptable level of after-sales support. Make sure that the supplier is well established and reputable, so that you can be sure of continued support. Will support be available outside normal office hours?

6   **Make sure your chosen system can run the software you need to use.** Seek assurances from prospective suppliers that the system they are offering will run all the software you intend to use. In particular, make sure that it includes enough memory to run the software at an acceptable speed. Systems can be fitted with extra memory later, but this tends to be expensive.

7   **Check the warranty that the machine will have.** The lengths and terms of warranties vary. Some are 'on-site', meaning that an engineer will come to your premises to carry out repairs. Some are 'back to base', meaning that the system will have to be returned to the supplier. Is any guarantee given about repair times?

8   **Continue to seek advice.** Even when you think you have a good idea of what you're going to purchase, continue to ask friends and colleagues for their opinions. Read articles in magazines and journals. Read some general computing books.

9   **Read the small print.** When you are comparing systems from different suppliers, check exactly what is being offered. Some companies will economise on some areas (eg hard disk speed or monitor quality) to offer a lower price. Don't forget to check whether VAT is included or not, and whether there are ways you can avoid having to pay it yourself.

10   **Do you want a network?** If you know that you will want to link several machines together to share data, printers etc, you need to consider the cost of networking. A few manufacturers include much of what you need for networking, so it may be worth buying from one of them.

11   **Be realistic about its useful life.** If you buy the latest computer now, it will be quite out of date in about three years. If you need to be fairly up-to-date with technology, your budgeting should allow for replacement of the system every three years or so.

12   **Be wary of the latest technology.** By definition, the newest technology is the least tried and tested, as well as the most expensive. Unless you really need it, let someone else have the expense and the risk of testing the latest flashy gizmos.

13   **Try to keep an eye on technology, so that you know what is possible.** New systems tend to be more powerful and easier to use. If you become set in your ways, you may not realise what is possible and so you could miss out on useful developments.

14   **Old computers still work as well as when they were new.** What happens is that the needs of the user tend to change. If you have an old computer, but you are perfectly happy with it, there is no need to change.

15   **Computers can often be upgraded.** If your computer is slow, or won't run some software, it may be possible to upgrade it. The simplest upgrade is to add more memory, but sometimes the processor can be changed. The most complex upgrade is a change of the 'motherboard' (the main electronic board inside your computer). This can effectively give you a new computer, but you may still be able to use some of the old components such as the case, disk drives, mouse and keyboard.

16   **Study the costs carefully before upgrading.** If you replace a series of components with more recent ones, it could cost you more than it would have done to sell your old system and buy a new one. Try to cost any upgrades fully before starting on the process.

17   **Buying a machine which can be upgraded can help you if your budget is limited.** You may be able to find machines advertised which are cheap because they don't meet current demands. If you could buy one of these and make do with its limitations in the short term, you could at least start computing. Some items, such as hard disks or additional memory are relatively cheap, but others, such as monitors, are expensive, so be careful. Check that a budget machine will be able to take modern graphics, sound and other expansion cards.

18   **Be wary about obsolete stock.** Sometimes very cheap computers are advertised. These were often perfectly good machines in their day, but that time has passed. Unless they can be upgraded economically, they are effectively in a dead end and will be unable to run current programs properly.

19   **Check whether software supplied as part of a deal is supplied on floppy disks or CD-ROM.** Many companies supply software pre-installed, but don't give you copies of the installation disks or CD-ROMs. This means that you have to backup your system to floppies so that you can re-install the software if you need to. You will need a large number of floppy disks for this (perhaps 30 or 40) and the backup process will take a long time. Make sure that you carry out the backup process if you need to, otherwise you will be in extreme difficulties if anything goes badly wrong.

20   **Compare several suppliers.** Once you have decided exactly what you want, contact several suppliers and compare their offers in detail. Compare price, exact specification (including software supplied), delivery time, after-sales support and warranties.

21   **Integrated computer systems can have pros and cons.** These systems have everything you need built into one box (apart from the keyboard). They often comprise monitor, disk drive, CD-ROM drive, modem and loudspeaker all in one unit. Their main advantages are that they are very simple to set up and all the components should work together effectively. The disadvantages are that they may be difficult to upgrade and that, in the event of a breakdown, they can be difficult to repair.

2

Making the purchase

Once you have decided exactly what to buy and who to buy it from, you may find it useful to heed the following suggestions before clinching your deal.

1   **Pay by credit card if possible.** This will give you added protection from the credit card company. Some credit cards even give you insurance for a limited period on items you buy with them.

2   **Check on the exact costs.** Make sure that delivery costs are taken into account. Check whether VAT is included in the price, or charged separately.

3   **Check that prices or specifications haven't changed.** Computers change so fast that it is quite possible that a model you see advertised one month will have undergone changes by the next month. These changes may be for the better, but they could be unwelcome changes in some feature that you had specially chosen.

4   **Don't be tempted by extras that you don't want.** Manufacturers often 'bundle' items with their systems to make them seem attractive. This is fine if you want these items, but they may be inappropriate (for example, one company's office suite of software when you want to use a different one). Make sure that these extras are not old versions which are no longer sellable, and so are being dumped on unsuspecting buyers.

5   **Negotiate the delivery date.** Some suppliers will take your money and then not complete the order for a long time. Ask if it is in stock, or how long it will take to arrive. If it is important that you don't have to wait, use the words 'Time is of the essence' on a written order. This adds the need for timely delivery to the contract.

6   **Ask whom you are speaking to and keep notes.** Hopefully you will have no problems, but if you are given information that turns out to be misleading, notes will be very useful in making a complaint. Start keeping such notes from the very first contact.

7   **Don't pay for express delivery unless you need to.** If you need a machine in a hurry, by all means pay. It is quite likely that you may have to wait until your machine is in stock anyway, so there is little point in paying extra delivery costs.

8   **Write 'Goods not inspected' on the delivery note.** All you will see on delivery is the outside of some large cardboard boxes, so protect yourself in case any of the contents are damaged or any items are missing.

9   **Check the delivery as soon as possible.** If there are any problems, contact the supplier immediately. If you are genuinely inconvenienced by missing or damaged items, ask for compensation.

10   **The Mail Order Protection Scheme may help you.** When you purchase by mail order from advertisements in many magazines, this scheme can be used if problems develop. The magazines will print information about it.

3

Cheap or free items

Buying a computer and all the associated bits and pieces can be very expensive. There are ways of saving money, particularly on programs (or software), which are worth investigating. See the section on viruses and take appropriate precautions.

1 **Some programs are given away free by their writers.** These are known as freeware. If you find one that you need, you can use it free of charge and without restriction. These programs are not common, as it takes time and effort to write programs. Some people believe that computing should be open to all and are prepared to give their work away. Some items distributed as freeware are surprisingly useful.

2 **Remember that shareware is not really free.** The programs are distributed free of charge, but should be registered if you continue to use them. The user can try the programs and, if they are useful, pay to register them. Registered users often gain benefits such as updated versions, manuals and access to support. Not only programs, but also fonts and clip art are available on a shareware basis.

3 **Some software is made freely available, but disabled in some way.** Often you will not be able to save or print your work, or perhaps only small files can be worked on, but you do have the opportunity to try the software to decide if you want to buy it.

4 **Major pieces of software are sometimes given away completely free, and are fully operational!** These are usually old versions and the strategy is to entice you to buy the latest product. These old versions can be perfectly satisfactory and the opportunity to upgrade to the latest version at a discount is often given.

5 **Artwork which you can use in your work is sold quite cheaply on a copyright-free basis.** This is often referred to as clip art. You can use these pictures to embellish your own work. Samples of more expensive clip art are sometimes given away, again to entice you to buy more.

6 **Look out for free fonts.** Font manufacturers sometimes give away complete fonts as a showcase to encourage you to buy more.

7 **Magazine cover disks and CD-ROMs can be a valuable source of goodies.** It is probably worth buying a CD-ROM drive just to try out a few from different magazines and to make use of the items offered there. Take care, though, to avoid cluttering up your hard disk.

8 **There are companies which sell freeware and shareware products.** They have extensive catalogues and you can find all manner of obscure programs in them. How can they charge for free software? They just charge for copying, distribution and administration — the programs are free. These companies advertise in magazines.

9 **If you have a modem, you can find software to download from bulletin boards or the Internet.** Check carefully about how much you have to pay as you can be paying premium-rate telephone charges. Take suitable precautions against importing viruses.

10 **Consumables such as paper, printer ribbons, inkjet printer cartridges and laser printer toner cartridges can be recycled.** Check for scrap paper around other people's computers as they only usually use one side. The other side is fine for rough copies. Ribbons can be re-inked and inkjet cartridges can be refilled very cheaply, but do this away from your computer as it can be messy. Some companies offer schemes to overhaul and refill toner cartridges at an appreciable saving.

4

Organising your workspace

People often sit at a computer for hours at a time and are surprised when they feel tired and have aches and pains afterwards. If you find you are unexpectedly tired or stressed after each session with your computer, take steps to put things right before they worsen. Most desks and chairs were designed for writing and are at the wrong height for computer use. If you can choose your furniture, bear in mind the points below. If, like most people, you have to use the desk and chair you are given, take steps to adapt it as far as possible.

1 **Make sure your monitor is at a suitable height.** As a general guide, the top should slightly below eye level. Working with the monitor too low is very common. This results in back and neck strain due to the weight of the head being unbalanced.

2 **Looking down at the keyboard causes neck and back strain.** If it is a serious problem, try to learn to touch type. There are computer programs available to help you with this and the time spent learning will soon be repaid.

3 **The keyboard should be at the correct height.** When you are typing, your forearms should be at about right angles to your upper arms and your wrists should be straight. An adjustable height chair can help achieve this. If you use a mouse, make sure your hand is relaxed when you use it. Ergonomic mice are available to help with this. Repetitive Strain Injuries (RSI) can result from working with bent wrists for prolonged periods. These injuries can be disabling and should be taken seriously.

4 **Your arms should be supported when you are typing** This can be done by an adjustable wristrest. If you haven't got one, experiment with a piece of wood wrapped up in some towelling or other thick material. If it helps, buy a proper rest.

5   **Make sure that your feet are flat on the floor.** If your knees are lower than your hips when the chair is at the correct height for everything else, use a footrest.

6   **When copying from a source document, have it in a good position.** Have it at the same level and distance as the screen to avoid looking up and down and refocusing all the time. Document holders are available for this purpose.

7   **Minimise eyestrain problems.** If you have headaches, or blurred vision or itchy eyes, see your optician. Contact lenses wearers should make a conscious effort to blink as computer use encourages staring at the screen, which can dry lenses out.

8   **Take care with reading glasses and bifocals.** These can cause problems with focusing on the screen. Bifocal wearers may suffer neck strain from tilting their heads. Your optician will be able to advise you and possibly prescribe special glasses for computing.

9   **Lighting is very important.** You must have good lighting to work effectively, but there shouldn't be any glare on the screen. Situate your computer so that you avoid reflections, or use screens to block light from the screen. Anti-glare screens are available to fit to the front of a monitor. A desk lamp can be useful as it can be adjusted according to your needs.

10   **Take plenty of rest breaks away from the computer.** Make sure you rest your eyes and body. Some simple stretching exercises can help. Try to plan your work to incorporate a variety of tasks and to avoid long, continuous spells at the keyboard.

5

Health and safety

There are risks in doing anything and using IT is no exception. There are some real hazards, and some hype. Common sense will help you to avoid most hazards, but there are some hidden dangers which you need to be aware of.

1   **All electrical devices are potentially dangerous.** If you suspect that your computer may have an electrical fault, seek expert help. Watch out for damaged leads, broken cases, unusual 'hot' smells and crackling or fizzing noises. If you are worried, switch it off at the wall socket and unplug it.

2   **Many computers, monitors and printers are heavy.** If you want to move one, check its weight carefully before you go too far. Move one component at a time and disconnect all leads to avoid tripping over them. Be particularly careful about steps when you are carrying something which blocks your view.

3   **Most computers have a large number of wires connected to them.** Make sure they are located so that they can't trip anybody up. Pulling a lead out of the computer can cause it to stop working and you could lose your work. If leads are a hazard, tie them up in a bundle and secure them out of the way. If your computer is against a wall, you could put up a narrow shelf just below desk height. All the leads and power supplies can be held on this shelf.

4   **Think about radiation emissions from monitors.** These have been a source of worry for many years, particularly in the case of pregnant women. There is a lack of proof about whether or not this is a real problem. Modern monitors are constructed to strict standards for radiation emissions to minimise any hazard to the user, but it has been suggested that they produce dangerous levels of

radiation from the rear. Until proof is established, it would be prudent to avoid risks as far as possible by checking the specifications for monitors and for pregnant women to avoid spending long periods near them.

5   **There have been reports of a link between computers and facial dermatitis.** This may also be linked to low humidity and the static electrical field generated by the monitor. If you have any problems of this kind, try using a humidifier and reducing static with anti-static rugs or carpets. There are also anti-static screens to fit to monitors to help with this.

6   **Check that monitors will not cause epilepsy.** People who suffer from photosensitive epilepsy can have attacks triggered by a flickering screen. Sufferers will almost certainly know about this problem and should avoid poor quality monitors that flicker.

7   **Beware of ozone.** This gas is highly desirable in the upper atmosphere, but acutely toxic to people. It can be given off by laser printers and photocopiers. New laser printers have filters fitted, but these can lose efficiency. Fortunately, ozone can usually be detected by smell, usually described as 'the smell of electricity'. If you have a laser printer (or photocopier) near you, make sure there is adequate ventilation. If you are concerned, check with the manufacturer about its maintenance schedule. If you are not happy, arrange to have the exhaust vented outside by an extractor fan.

8   **Remember that toner used by laser printers can be hazardous.** Check the manufacturer's safety guidance before changing a toner cartridge and avoid any contact with the toner. Use disposable plastic gloves to provide extra protection.

9   **Cleaning materials used on computer equipment can cause allergic reactions.** Follow the health and safety rules on packaging carefully. Once again, disposable plastic gloves will provide extra protection.

10 **Don't hit your computer, however justified you may feel!** It will hurt you more than it hurts the computer. Invest in a foam brick to throw against the wall!

6

'Green' issues

There are many environmental issues related to computers. Some suppliers are already attempting to address these issues, so if you ask questions about them it will encourage manufacturers to continue their efforts. It is impossible to consider all the issues, but these are a start:

1   **Ask about manufacturing methods.** Solvents are widely used in the manufacture of electronic goods. Some solvents damage the environment. Some manufacturers use alternative, safer solvents as part of their 'green' policies.

2   **Check up on power consumption.** Computer systems vary considerably in the amount of power required to operate them. Additionally, many systems will 'power down' into a low power consumption mode when they are left unused, coming back to life when the mouse is moved, or a key is pressed. These systems can be configured to suit your needs. If you are using a screen saver, make sure that it does not prevent the computer from shutting down by requiring disk access or processor activity.

3   **Ask about recyclable components.** Some manufacturers design their computers and peripherals (printers, and so on) so that, when their useful life is over, they can be returned to them and the raw materials can be re-used.

4   **What about packaging?** Are packaging materials recycled, or biodegradable? (Bear in mind that it may be useful to keep packaging in case you need to return the system for repair, or in case you need to transport it.)

5   **Find out about chemicals used for cleaning.** Chemical cleaners are available for screens, disk drives and other parts of a system. Are they safe and environmentally sound?

6 **Enquire about recycled or refilled materials.** Recycled paper is widely available (but is it bleached with chlorine?), and it is also possible to find ink for refilling printer cartridges and to buy serviced and refilled laser printer toner cartridges.

7 **Consider setting up a paperless office.** All sorts of information (drafts of papers or books, accounts, memos, letters) can be stored on disk rather than being printed out. Your computer system can send faxes or e-mail without using paper. But remember to keep backup copies of everything separately (and retrievably!).

8 **Consider how your computer system can save you journeys.** For example, if you can link from home to computers and printers at your institution or workplace, you may be able to arrange to work from home at agreed times, but still be able to communicate effectively with colleagues or students. You can also use electronic mail and computer conferencing to communicate without time restrictions.

9 **Think about providing students with materials already on computer disk.** This can save the costs of printing handouts, and can allow students the facility to edit and personalise the notes you supply them with.

10 **How long will the system last?** For many systems, the main environmental impact is during their manufacture. All machines will become out of date, but the longer it lasts, the less the damage to the environment (and your pocket!).

7

Panic page (technophobia)

Even the most experienced computer users will have major problems once in a while. It is easy to feel total panic when something goes wrong (normally stable people often cry!), but if you keep a clear head, you may be able to avert disaster.

1   **My work has all disappeared from the screen!** Make sure you haven't accidentally scrolled down or across the page. Have you started a new document by accident? Have you moved to a different spreadsheet workbook? If so, your work is there, but you can't see it. Check the scroll bars and try moving to different windows.

2   **My system won't work at all!** Check the obvious things first. Make sure it is plugged in and the socket is switched on. Is the socket working? Will another machine work from the same socket? If so, has the fuse in the plug blown? Has the screen illumination accidentally been turned right down? If there is no life at all after checking these, you may have a serious problem.

3   **The computer seems to work, but there is nothing on the monitor!** Is it plugged in and switched on? Monitors often take their power from a socket in the back of the computer and these connectors sometimes come loose. Is the signal lead (the other lead from the monitor) plugged in to the computer? If these all fail, is there another monitor (of the same type) that you could try on your computer, to find out whether it is the monitor or the computer which is at fault?

4   **My keyboard/mouse won't work!** Make sure they are plugged in! If they still won't work, can you try someone else's on your machine?

5   **My computer gives an error message when it starts up!** Have you left a disk in the floppy drive? If so, the computer will try to use instructions on it to control how it operates. If the disk is not a 'boot' disk which has been specially formatted, it won't work.

6   **My work won't print out!** Try the obvious things, like leads and power switches. Is the printer full of paper? Have you got a paper jam? Has the printer got toner or ink? If you are on a network, are you printing to the correct printer? Is the network working? Have you got enough memory left on your hard disk for printing to occur? When hard disks get too full, failure to print is sometimes the first warning you get.

7   **My computer reports problems with the hard disk or memory when it starts up!** Write down the message on a piece of paper so that you can report exactly what has happened. You will probably need professional help – or rather, your computer will need this!

8   **Is there anything else I can do before having my computer taken away for repair?** If you are of a practical (and brave) nature, you could take the lid off your computer and make sure that nothing has worked loose inside it. Before you start, make sure you are not charged up with static electricity by touching an earthed metal object (such as a radiator pipe). Check that leads are connected tightly and that memory modules are seated properly. If there are any chips on the computer board that are in sockets, make sure they are properly seated. Don't use excessive force and don't guess where any loose leads go (there are often a few spare leads inside a computer anyway). If in doubt, leave it alone, especially if it is still under guarantee.

9   **My machine needs to go away for repair and it has sensitive data on its hard disk!** This could be a problem. If it isn't a disk problem, can the hard disk be removed before sending it away? Speak to whoever is going to repair it and seek advice.

10 **My computer has gone off to be repaired and I need some work that's on it!** Use your backup disks on another computer. That's what they are for. What do you mean, you 'didn't think you needed to bother'? What will you do if the problem is a hard disk failure?

Chapter 2   Getting Started With Software

In this chapter, we provide suggestions for putting your equipment to work. You probably already know that the best way to get started with new software tends to be learning-by-doing, rather than to try to read all about it before ever giving it a try. You may also have found that a very important part of learning-by-doing is to get things wrong, and learn from each mistake. Of course, the aim needs to be to get things wrong at the right time – not when you're trying urgently to get things done with your new program.

You may be new to using some of the software types we've touched on, but there's every chance that you're already familiar with at least some kinds of software. In either case, we hope that you'll find some of our suggestions helpful. We know ourselves that even when we think we've mastered a software package, we often learn (usually from colleagues or students rather than the thick manuals which come with the packages) shortcuts and refinements which we would never have found by ourselves. We've tried to pass on some of these in this chapter.

Our first two sets of suggestions are generic: 'Learning to use a new program' and 'Where to find help'. These are aimed at readers who really are using software for the first time, and we don't expect experienced readers to need our suggestions here.

We move next to word processing. Many computer users want nothing more from their systems. Such users include writers whose primary rationale for having a system is to enable them to produce print, whether handouts, lecture notes, magazine articles, newsletters, contributions to learned journals, books such as this, or the best-selling novel that is supposed to lie dormant inside most of us! We've tried to divide our suggestions into two sets of ten, the first for getting the hang of the central principles of word processing, and the second for adding a bit of polish and sophistication should you need, or wish to.

Next we consider spreadsheets. If you've only ever used your computer for word processing, you may find this a significant leap. However, it is like learning any foreign language: once you've got the basic vocabulary, the learning curve flattens out (even if it's a very long curve). Again, we've divided our suggestions into two sets, the first for new starters.

Fewer people are involved in creating databases than in word processing or using spreadsheets. However, if your work is such that creating your own databases will save you lots of time, patience and energy in the long run, it is never too early to start playing with putting one together. If you have not been involved with databases, scanning our suggestions may seem like reading a foreign language at first, but once you start trying them out, we think you'll find that there is in fact a lot of satisfaction to be gained by creating and maintaining your own databases.

We continue with some suggestions about desktop publishing. If you're not into spreadsheets or databases, these follow logically from our tips about word processing. However, if you are also using spreadsheets or databases, you are almost certain to want to print out things deriving from them, and that's why we have placed our desktop publishing suggestions here. We continue with ideas on computer graphics, which can enhance many desktop-published products, and often are much easier to incorporate than you may have thought.

We end this chapter with three related sets of suggestions, on 'Data communications', 'Networking' and 'Getting to know the Internet'. For many readers, electronic communication may well be the main purpose of buying or using computers, and such readers may wish to start this chapter here. For other readers, these final sections may be of no interest whatsoever, especially if you're not linked up to networks and have no wish or need to become so. Ascending the learning curve of electronic communication can be done by starting directly to play with it, but can also be done by developing skills with word processing, spreadsheets, databases, and other software. In any case, for many users, the opportunity to link up electronically is not available all the time, and such applications may only be available to you at work, or if you are prepared to pay more in telephone bills — often a result of being linked-up at home. Our suggestions on electronic communication in this chapter are just for starters; it is a very big — and rapidly developing — field, and there are lots of magazines and books devoted solely to the topic. We hope we may help you in taking the first few steps at least.

8

Learning to use a new program

With modern computers, once you have learned to use one program, you will recognise many features in other programs. For example, you will probably find that many of the headings in the menu bar are the same on all the programs you use. This means that many common operations, such as loading, saving or printing your work are very easy and familiar when you start learning a new program.

1   **Allow enough time**. Learning to use a program can be very time consuming. Be prepared to invest some time in learning the program thoroughly. This will mean that you save time when you use the program in the future.

2   **Use tutorials.** Most programs come with tutorial materials and these are an obvious starting point. Usually these are hands-on interactive sequences which lead you step by step through the main features of the program. Their quality varies, but if nothing else, they will give you an overview of what is possible.

3   **Don't try to learn too much.** Modern programs are often extremely complex and many users will only ever use a small part of them. Work out which parts will be useful to you and learn them. Keep a mental note of what else is available, however, because you might need more facilities in the future.

4   **Find a 'real' task to try.** Tutorials can be very helpful, but you will only start to learn to use the program properly when you try to use it for a task of your own choosing. Trying to complete your own tasks will help focus your learning and will force you to confront new problems.

5   **Choose your tasks carefully.** Don't be too ambitious about what you can achieve in the early stages. Try to select tasks that will be based on what you already know, but which will also require you to develop some new skills.

6   **Don't be afraid to experiment.** If you want to try something new, go ahead! The worst you can do is to destroy all the work you have just done. Your computer will survive, though your temper may not!

7   **Save your work often.** If you save your work before trying anything new, and use a new number on the end of the filename, you can reload your work in the event of a disaster, thus virtually eliminating all risks.

8   **Practise regularly.** Like all skills, using a computer program well takes practice, particularly in the early stages. Try to keep using programs regularly so that you don't forget too much between sessions.

9   **Find out about Undo facilities.** Many programs allow you to undo the last thing you did, or even to undo a series of operations. You can also often Redo things. These facilities give you even greater freedom to experiment.

10 **Review your knowledge.** When you have used a program for a while, and you feel comfortable with it, review the skills you learnt at the beginning. You may well find, in the light of your experience, that you can see more effective methods of work. You may also now understand areas that you skimmed at the beginning. Your program may have a Quick Preview or Examples and Demos as part of its Help facility. Look at these occasionally, to make sure you are making the most of your program. Things you ignored when you first started with the program (for example, 'short cuts') may make a lot of sense once you are experienced enough to make use of them.

9

Where to find help

If you are learning to use computers on your own, it is easy to feel isolated. There is help available and someone else has probably solved the problem that you are struggling with. All you need to do is to find the help!

1   **Build up your own help notes.** As you are learning to use new programs or new machines, you'll learn so much that it is easy to forget important steps if you have not written them down somewhere. It can take ages to backtrack to where you found key instructions. It could be worth having a small notebook, where you jot down things that you are particularly keen to be able to find again quickly.

2   **Look in the Help section.** There is normally on-line help available within programs. Find out where it is and how to use it. Help facilities often include demonstrations of how to carry out tasks. There may also be other forms of help available, such as a 'tips' window or help 'balloons'. Find out how to turn them on and off as they can be annoying as well as being a benefit.

3   **Look in the manual.** Computer manuals are notorious for their complexity, but many programs come with a 'Getting Started' manual which is targeted at beginners. The full manual may be large and intimidating, but it will contain a vast amount of vital information. Start to use it at once so that you have some familiarity with its contents and layout.

4   **Find a book.** The complexity of computer manuals has resulted in the publication of books on all aspects of computer use. Many of these are targeted at novices and leave out the more complex information. You may find some of these books insulting in tone

(particularly the American ones), but they can be helpful. These books are often expensive, so try to borrow one from a library or from a colleague.

5   **Read a magazine.** Newsagents' shelves are bursting with a huge array of computing magazines. Some of these are very good and it is worth investigating them. They are very up-to-date and are the best source of current information. They are often packed with advertisements, but this keeps the price down to a reasonable level. Find one that is at the correct level (i.e. it teaches you something, but isn't too advanced) and consider subscribing to it.

6   **Try a video-based or computer-based training package.** These are available for computers in general, and for a wide range of programs. They can be quite expensive and they don't suit everybody, but if you can find one, try it and see if it helps.

7   **Ask for help.** If you know someone who uses the program you want to learn, make contact with them. It is probably better to have some specific questions for them – 'Do you know how to...', rather than just saying 'Will you teach me to use X'. You will be respected for having tried for yourself before seeking help.

8   **Start a 'self-help' group.** Test out the old saying that 'Two heads are better than one'. If you can find other people who are in the same position as yourself to discuss problems with, you may all be able to supply different pieces of the jigsaw. This kind of help may also be available via the Internet, but will usually be very advanced as novice users may find the Internet difficult.

9   **Teach someone else.** It may sound bizarre, but this will force you to examine your knowledge and you may gain sudden enlightenment while explaining something to someone else. It will also let you see the tasks that this person is attempting and it may spark off new ideas for your own future work.

10 **Go on a course.** Take advantage of any training that is available. There may be 'in-house' training available, or a local college may offer a suitable course. Commercial computer courses can be expensive, but if they save you enough time, they may be worth the money.

10

First steps with word processors

Word processors are the most familiar computer application. At their simplest, they are just sophisticated typewriters, allowing the user to check text before printing out. They are capable of far more than this, however, and it is worth learning how to use some of their other facilities.

1   **Explore your options for selecting text.** The mouse is the most common tool for selecting text, for example to copy, or move, or delete. Find out about using extra techniques, such as double clicking text, clicking in margins or using different mouse buttons. These can often help you to work faster.

2   **Avoid replacing text accidentally.** If you *select* some text, it will be replaced by anything you type. This can result in text disappearing by accident, so take care. If this happens, you may be able to undo the operation and recover the lost typing – but you may not be able to retrieve the masterful phrase you typed in before instructing 'undo'!

3   **Experiment with your options for formatting text.** When you have selected some text, it can be formatted. You can change fonts and sizes and colour, embolden or italicise it. You can also align it differently on the page (for example, it can be centred) and with many word processors you can adjust the spaces between characters and lines. Try to avoid too many fonts and effects in a document or it may look very untidy.

4   **Get familiar with Cut, Copy and Paste.** Selected text can be cut or copied and then pasted into another place. This is useful for making amendments, but it can also help if you need to enter some text repeatedly. Some word processors let you move text by highlighting it and then dragging it to a new place. If these operations can be carried out from the keyboard, it is worth learning to do this as it will save time.

5   **Practise inserting or removing headers and footers.** These can be added automatically to the top or bottom of each page of your document. Page numbers, the date, the time and other items can also be added.

6   **Explore any options you may have for numbering and bulleting paragraphs or sections.** Not all programs give you such options. However, some programs allow your paragraphs to be automatically numbered in a range of styles. Bullets are symbols at the left of paragraphs to highlight key points. Note that these characters cannot usually be deleted – you need to highlight the paragraph and use the appropriate menu to remove the bullets or numbers.

7   **Check out any options you have to make borders.** With some programs you can put borders around paragraphs by highlighting them first. You can choose whether a complete box is added or whether just some lines will be included in the box. You can also change the style and thickness of the lines used for the borders, and sometimes draw 'patterned' lines.

8   **Explore your options for showing and hiding non-printing characters.** Some of the keys you press (such as the space bar, return key and tab key) do not produce characters that appear in a printout. They can cause problems sometimes (particularly a return in the wrong place). Most word processors allow you to make them temporarily visible, which can be very useful if you are having problems with the layout of your text.

9   **Use the tab key for indenting text.** Most word processors use fonts which vary the space according to the character being typed (proportional fonts). If you use spaces to indent text, correct alignment on the screen may be impossible and the alignment will change when it is printed out. Use the tab key instead and learn to set tabs where you want them.

10   **Make the most of any spell checking facilities.** A spell checking program can spot errors that you have missed and is worth using. Bear in mind, however, that it cannot spot missing or wrong words as it merely checks that words exist. Many word processors allow you to define long (or difficult to spell) words and enter them automatically by pressing a few keys. This is particularly useful if you use a lot of technical, legal, medical or similar terms.

11

Where to go next with word processors

Word processors are, for many computer users, the most used package. Many tasks can be carried out satisfactorily using basic facilities, but there are many extras that will increase productivity and improve the quality of your finished documents.

1   **Define your styles.** If you are producing a long, report-style document, it is hard to be consistent about the style (font, size, alignment) of all the different headings, subheadings and the body of the text. You can with some programs define 'styles' to apply to these so that they will automatically be consistent.

2   **Try inserting pictures, diagrams and charts.** Most word processors allow you to insert objects into the text. You can then place text around them. Some packages include simple drawing facilities.

3   **Check options for using symbols and 'foreign' characters.** If you regularly use a foreign language, or scientific symbols, it is worth investigating how to do this. Most word processors can produce a much wider range of characters than are available directly from the keyboard. There are fonts available designed to allow you to put symbols into your text. You can view a table showing you the symbols available in any font. You may be able to access more by using an extra key (such as the alt key). Some machines allow you to use a menu at any time to check what symbols are available with each key.

4   **Use tables effectively.** Defining a table can be much easier than using the tab key to arrange text in tabular format. Don't forget that you may need to allow a row or column for headings (you can

usually add them later anyway). Adding borders to a table can make it look very tidy.

5   **Develop your word processing strategy.** When you are happy with the basic operation of your word processor, you should be able to develop your writing methods. Because it is so easy to alter your text, you can try techniques such as writing the headings first, then filling them out and having an 'ideas' area in your document for quick notes for later development. Mark unfinished areas with a symbol (such as ***) and you can search for the symbol later to find these sections.

6   **Explore any Outliners options.** These are included as part of many word processors. They allow you to set up headings and subheadings which are automatically formatted. You can promote and demote headings or change the order of headings and the relevant text will move with the headings.

7   **Check whether you can customise your word processor.** It is often possible to change the menu system, the toolbars and even the keyboard to suit your needs. For most people, the standard facilities are fine, but many more commands are available than can be accessed from the menus. If you need extra ones, you can set up the package the way you want it.

8   **Try out mail merging.** You can type a document and then use the data in a database to add some details automatically. This can be a great time saver if you need to produce slight variations on a basic document, for example, letters with different names and addresses. The computer can even use criteria to select which copies to produce.

9   **Experiment with file exchange options.** Most word processors can convert files written with other packages into their own particular formats, and allow you to save your own files in alternative formats. These options can make it possible to exchange files with other people working with different packages. (To write this book we used two different packages and machines!)

10   **Don't stop learning!** Even when you're experienced with a word processing package, it can be well worthwhile having someone else looking over your shoulder as you work with it (and vice versa). You'll often be pleasantly surprised by tips and wrinkles other people can alert you to (especially students!).

12

First steps with spreadsheets

Spreadsheets are programs which organise and manipulate numbers. They were originally intended for accountancy, but are valuable for a much wider range of uses. The principles are very simple. Numbers are entered in rows and columns, and headings are added to label items. Each location on the spreadsheet is called a cell. Formulae are then entered to carry out operations on the numbers. When it is required to carry out the same operations on different sets of figures, formulae can usually be copied, saving time and thought. If numbers are changed, recalculation is automatic and very quick. Operations on the numbers can be as simple as adding numbers together, but there is scope for enormous levels of complexity. The following tips should help you learn the first steps in a sensible order.

1   **Plan your work.** It is easy to leave out a column, or forget to allow a row for headings. Spreadsheets are very flexible and it is fairly easy to correct mistakes in the layout of your work, but learn to do this later. A few minutes with some scrap paper will reduce problems.

2   **Check out your arithmetic first.** Spreadsheets will calculate for you, but you must tell them what to do. Work out how to do the calculations on paper and check some results so that you can make sure your spreadsheet is giving you the correct answers. This is particularly important if you are not good at arithmetic!

3   **Use the keyboard as much as possible.** The mouse is very useful for many tasks, but if you keep switching between the mouse and the keyboard, it will slow you down. In particular, data entry can usually be done without the mouse.

4   **Use the numeric keypad.** Most keyboards have a numeric keypad which is designed for entering numbers. Try to use this, rather than the numbers across the top of the keyboard. It will be quicker if you practise and the arithmetic signs are there too. If the cursor moves when you try to use this keypad, press the key labelled Num Lock if your keyboard has one.

5   **Don't worry if columns are too narrow.** If an item (such as a long heading) doesn't fit in a column, don't worry. The computer can still use it and you can find out how to change column widths later.

6   **Play with simple numbers first.** Get your spreadsheet to do operations that you can check at a glance, such as subtracting, adding, multiplying or squaring.

7   **Check how much precision you need.** You can usually control how many significant figures you wish your answers to be calculated to. There's no point having eight significant figures if all you want is a round estimate.

8   **Don't panic if all your data disappears.** The screen only shows you a small part of the space available for your work. It is possible that you have accidentally scrolled to an empty part of the spreadsheet. Check the row and column numbers and go back to the top left corner. If your program uses workbooks, you could have changed to a different sheet by accident. Make sure you are on sheet 1.

9   **Check out your print options.** When a spreadsheet is bigger than can be printed out onto a single sheet, you may need to work out how best to print it out in instalments, each with appropriate headings, page numbers and so on. Many spreadsheets are wider than they are long, so it may be better to print them in 'landscape' mode.

10   **Make sure your finished spreadsheet looks good.** It is easy to embolden important items, to change fonts, add borders and even to use colour. This can make a very simple spreadsheet look good, but keep it tasteful! Bear in mind that you might not be able to print in colour.

13

Where to go next with spreadsheets

Once you feel comfortable with the fundamentals of your spreadsheet, you can start to explore some of the more complex features.

1   **Explore the built-in functions in your spreadsheet program.** Simple arithmetic is the best starting point for learning about spreadsheets, but built-in functions are included for many common tasks. For example, you can produce an average of a column of figures using arithmetic, but there will be a function to do this automatically. Most of the functions are simple, but some are quite complex. Use the ones which sound familiar first, such as Max, which returns the largest value in a range of numbers. Avoid the complex sounding ones, such as Hypgeomdist, unless you have some idea what they mean and you need them.

2   **Use the correct format for numbers.** Spreadsheets allow you to format numbers by changing the number of decimal places shown, adding currency symbols and adding percentage signs. If your data isn't being displayed the way you want it, change it!

3   **Learn how to produce charts from your spreadsheets.** It is simple to produce good pie, bar, line and other charts from your spreadsheets. These can be useful for presentations and for teaching. They can also be pasted into word-processed documents for reports.

4   **Find out how to change the layout of your spreadsheets.** Even if you plan your work carefully, you will find it very useful to be able to add or delete rows and columns, change the widths of columns and to move data and formulae to different locations. This can be very useful when you decide to adapt an existing spreadsheet for a new task.

5   **Reuse your spreadsheets as much as possible.** If you use your spreadsheet program regularly for a task, save a 'template' version, with headings and formulae in place, but without the data. You can then load the template, add the data and the results will be produced. Make sure you don't destroy the template when you save the version which includes the data.

6   **Learn to use absolute cell references.** This sounds complicated, but it will pay dividends to learn about it and it isn't really very hard. You have already used relative cell references, without realising it! Absolute cell references are used so that the contents of a cell can be used in a formula and will still be correct wherever the formula is copied to. Try examples in manuals, books and help files until you understand it and can do it.

7   **Think of useful applications regarding your teaching.** For example, you may be able to use spreadsheets to store students' marks for coursework on an ongoing basis, and to print out class lists of marks, and to do the final computations combining their coursework and exam results.

8   **Use help from colleagues who have more experience.** But don't let them just give you a template they've designed; ask them to help you to make one of your own. That way, you'll find it much easier to adapt it and develop it to suit your own needs.

9   **Don't forget to label histograms and charts properly.** The spreadsheet program will usually produce good diagrams, but you need to add captions and label axes well for other people to understand them easily.

10 **Tell other people about your uses of spreadsheets.** Many people still continue to do tedious computations by long-winded methods. Spread the word about the power of the computer to save on boring work!

14

First steps with databases

Database programs are used to store, manipulate and retrieve data. At their simplest level, they are the electronic equivalent of file card systems. Because the data is stored electronically, however, it is possible to perform tasks which are difficult with a manual system, such as extracting all the data that meets certain criteria or sorting the data into a different order. More sophisticated uses of databases might involve several files linked together with a menu so that a user could carry out complex tasks by simply choosing options. Database programs used to be concerned with textual and numeric data, but modern programs can handle pictures, sounds or any other data type.

1   **Plan ahead.** Before you start to construct a new database, design its structure on paper. Although it is possible to go back and alter the design when it is on the computer, it will be quicker to do it correctly the first time.

2   **Choose field names carefully.** If field names are too long and descriptive, they will make your design untidy and fill your screen with clutter. On the other hand, if they are too cryptic, you may have trouble remembering what they are if you go back to them six months later.

3   **Use the correct field type.** Database programs use a wide range of field types. Give some thought to using the correct type so that you can enter your data easily and achieve the results you need. For example, numbers can be entered into text fields but you will not be able to use them for calculations, so you should use a numeric field.

4   **Use choice fields whenever possible.** Choice fields let you enter data by selecting it from a list. If a field only has a limited range of possibilities (such as Sex – Male or Female are the only acceptable

entries), restricting data entry to a list of choices will reduce errors. If the choices available are long (or difficult to spell), typing will also be easier.

5 **Think about how your data will be updated.** A good example of the problems that can arise is the use of an age field. It may be correct when it is entered, but a year later, all the entries will be wrong. It is far better to use a date of birth field and get the computer to calculate the age for you.

6 **Design your data entry screen carefully.** When the user is entering data, it is confusing if the cursor jumps around the screen as fields are filled. Ideally, the cursor should move straight down a single column. If there are too many fields for this, fill one column before starting the other, or use two screens for data entry.

7 **Be careful when entering data.** If you are not a touch-typist and are not watching the screen, it is easy to enter data into the wrong field. This is a particular problem if the cursor moves on automatically when a field is full, but you don't realise it has done so and you press the return key.

8 **Make sure you include the correct fields.** The main purpose of a database is to output data in the form you want it, when you want it. In order to do this, you must store the correct data so that it can be manipulated, so don't leave any fields out. Conversely, don't store data that you will never need.

9 **Think about the format of your output.** It can be difficult to fit all the data you want on printer paper satisfactorily. Try different formats, such as using columns, using one field per line or using the same layout as you used for data entry. Do you need all the fields you are printing? After you have struggled to produce good layouts a few times, you will appreciate the benefits of short field names.

10 **Use quick reporting methods until you are familiar with database principles.** Many programs allow you to produce reports by showing an example of how your report is to work. These methods are a good introduction to databases, but be aware that you will need to tackle programming your database if your needs become more sophisticated.

15

Where to go next with databases

1   **Learn about related tables.** The power of databases is increased
    enormously by linking files (or tables) together. One of the main
    purposes of this is to avoid duplicated (or redundant) data. Another
    purpose is to cope with variable amounts of data. Unfortunately, this
    topic tends to sound complicated. If you are using databases and
    you are finding the logic complicated, persevere and do tutorial
    exercises on linking tables together. It isn't as hard as it sounds at
    first.

2   **Avoid redundant data.** As an example, consider a database of
    products which includes a supplier's name, address and other details
    for each item. As soon as there are two items from the same supplier,
    there will be duplicated data. Another major problem is the work
    and the scope for errors that would arise if the supplier were to
    change address. The solution is to store the products in one file and
    the supplier information in another. A supplier code is entered for
    each product and the computer can look up the supplier details from
    the second file.

3   **Related tables again!** These are so important that another tip is
    warranted! Imagine a database is storing the details of customers
    (name, address, etc) and a list of the items they have bought. There
    is an obvious problem here – how many fields should be used for
    the items bought? They won't all buy the same number of items, and
    there could be hundreds of them. Use one file for the customers and
    include a field in which to store a unique number for each customer.
    Use a second file for details of the products that have been bought
    and include the appropriate customer number for each item. Now

the computer can link the two files together to extract the information in the form that is required.

4 **Son of related tables.** If you have large numbers of linked files, the situation can become very complex. There are procedures for correctly designing such a database. If you find yourself in this situation, find out how it should be done properly. If you are looking for a suitable book, check in the index to see if it covers normalisation of databases.

5 **Learn to write procedures.** Programs can be written to automate database tasks. This is particularly useful if you need to carry out some functions repeatedly (for example, producing a monthly report). These procedures can be saved and reloaded for use at a later date.

6 **Investigate non-textual data.** You can store pictures, sounds and even movies with many database programs. These are not needed by most users, but you might find them useful. Because they involve large amounts of data, they will increase your storage requirements and may slow the operation of your system.

7 **Producing charts and graphs.** If it would be useful, see if you can produce charts to help summarise your data.

8 **Free-form databases are available.** These are designed to work with unstructured text files and will enable you to carry out qualitative analysis of the data.

9 **Design custom menu systems.** Most database programs allow you to produce your own menu systems to automate a complete application. These can allow inexperienced users to carry out tasks you have designed for them without risk to your data.

10 **Compile your complete application.** At the top end of database work, you can turn your complete application into a self-contained program that will run without need for the database program. This can mean very fast operation. Testing needs to be thorough before this is done.

16

Desktop publishing

Desktop publishing programs enable you to produce documents ready for publishing. This doesn't sound very different to word processing and as word processors increase in complexity, they are becoming capable of many desktop publishing tasks. A good desktop publishing program will, however, give you good control over how your document looks.

1 **Use your word processor to type your documents.** Desktop publishing programs include story editors which enable you to type your text, but it is probably better to use your word processor, with its familiar facilities, to type your text. You can then import the text into your desktop publisher.

2 **Use your desktop publisher for page layout.** This area is where these programs excel. They include facilities for aligning blocks of text exactly, and may let you rotate blocks of text.

3 **Import graphics and 'flow' text around them.** You can place images anywhere in your document and control the way that the accompanying text is shaped around the pictures.

4 **Learn to use master pages.** These pages control all the text and formatting that will appear throughout your document. These include headers and footers and also the margins. You can define left and right pages to allow the correct margins for binding the pages.

5 **Be tasteful.** You will be able to use a wide range of fonts, sizes, styles and effects. Experiment with them, but don't use too many in a document, and make sure it is clear and easily readable.

6 **Link documents together to form books.** Long documents are hard to handle. Many desktop publishing packages allow you to work in smaller blocks, then link them together to form a book.

7   **Let the system help you compile your contents page.** Many systems will allow you to collect together lists of headings and subheadings, and some will even automatically give you the page numbers.

8   **Let the system help you make an index.** Some systems will tell you what the most frequently occurring keywords are, and where they occur in your text.

9   **If you need high quality prints, contact a bureau.** These companies will be able to take your file and print it to the level of quality that you need. They will have equipment and expertise that would be very expensive to develop yourself. Speak to them at an early stage to find out exactly what they need from you.

10 **Consider using a larger monitor.** If you are doing a lot of page layout work, you will probably find a normal monitor inconvenient. An A4 monitor will enable you to see a complete A4 page at once. You could even consider an A3 monitor, to allow you to see a two page spread. These monitors are expensive, but you could save money by using a monochrome (or black and white) monitor.

17

Specialist software

The variety of specialist software is mindbending! In the following notes, our intention is simply to alert you to a few possibilities amid a vast range of options.

1 **Special software is available for project management.** Planning that is done using Gantt and Pert charts, and other techniques, can be done very effectively using this software.

2 **Flowcharting software can be very useful.** These programs include special flowcharting symbols and make it easy to link them together to form complex charts. If the symbols you require are not all included, you can draw your own.

3 **If you use statistics regularly, look for a specialist package.** Spreadsheets and other numeric packages include many statistical functions and are adequate for many people, but programs designed with statistics as their primary function will do much more, and be more efficient.

4 **If you can't find a program to do what you want, you could write your own!** This is not a task to be undertaken lightly, but millions of people worldwide do it! Quite a few visual programming languages are available now, and these use the graphic-user interface to help perform sophisticated tasks with comparative ease. Before deciding to become a programmer, search very hard in case someone else has already written the program you need!

5 **Morphing software changes one image into another.** If you provide a starting image and a final image, the computer can produce a series of intermediate frames which can be displayed as a 'movie'. You will also need to identify which points in the original picture will become which points in the new picture.

6   **If you travel by road frequently, route planning can be very useful.** If you enter the start point and the destination, the computer can produce a number of routes for you to choose from. You can also specify stop-off points and control preferences such as whether or not you like using motorways. The program will also indicate how long the journey will take (traffic permitting!) and will work out costs.

7   **Bar code technology is not restricted to shops.** Bar code readers are relatively cheap, and software is available to print the codes and to read them. If you need to distribute and collect large amounts of data, such technology could help you.

8   **Don't struggle with entering complex mathematical formulae.** Special software is available for this, either as part of a word processing package, or as a specialist program. Some of these programs will perform calculations and produce graphs as well. They can handle Bessel and Euler functions, Fast Fourier Transforms, and have a host of other facilities.

9   **Personal Information Managers can help you organise your life.** These include facilities such as a diary, a simple card-file database, and a notepad. Some include network support as well. However, no such program is guaranteed to make you better organised – you still have some choice!

10   **Your computer can keep track of all your contacts.** Programs called Contact Managers will help you to do this. They can store names, addresses, phone, fax and e-mail details and link to your word processor. They vary greatly in the facilities they offer, so compare them carefully before you choose one. They can be similar to Personal Information Managers, but a good one is based around each one of your contacts, rather than around you.

18

Computer graphics

If you need to produce charts or drawings, you can use your computer. You can then incorporate the results into your word-processed documents, or use them to help you make presentations at meetings.

1 **Check out presentation managers.** If you need to produce a series of pages (or slides) that you can present in turn, each using the same layout, this could be what you need. You can select background styles, effects, colours and headings for all the slides. You can then add text (bulleted, if you like), charts and graphics to the individual slides. You can print the result (onto OHP transparencies, perhaps) or use the computer screen to give a slide show.

2 **Add sound and movies to your presentations.** If you have music and moving image files, you can play them from your presentation manager.

3 **Practise your presentation.** Presentation managers often have facilities to help you keep track of the timing of your presentations. They may also allow you to produce versions of the slides with notes on them which you can use to help give a well-organised presentation.

4 **Try out charting packages.** These packages enable you to produce organisation charts, flowcharts, Venn diagrams and other charts. The results can often be imported into other packages such as word processors or presentation managers.

5 **Painting packages can be useful.** These programs let you 'paint' on the screen. Even if you have no artistic talent, you may be able to use one to produce something useful. They are very intuitive to use and the Undo facility is very useful.

6 **Drawing packages are useful for simple technical graphics.** These programs let you draw shapes on the screen. A range of pre-defined shapes are available and can be used to construct more complex items.

7 **Learn the difference between painting and drawing.** Painting packages colour individual pixels (dots) on the screen, according to your actions with the mouse (or other drawing device). The computer stores the exact details of every pixel on the screen. You will be able to draw circles, boxes and other shapes and you can change the width of the lines. A 'rubber' is included so that you can clear pixels from the screen. Drawing packages work in a different way. When you draw a line, the computer stores instructions about how that line is created. You cannot use a 'rubber' tool to delete the middle of a line. All the shapes on the screen are objects, and operations such as deletion are carried out on these objects.

8 **If you can't draw what you want, look for something to edit.** You may be able to make a few adjustments to an existing graphic to match it to your needs. Be careful about the copyright of the original graphic.

9 **Experiment with computer-aided design.** There are programs available which let you do detailed design work on your computer. These have many advantages over hand designing methods, such as ease of correcting, simple modifications to designs, the ability to copy repeated design elements and easy scaling. They can even work out costings if they are linked to databases. These programs can be very complex and so you will need to invest some time into learning them.

10 **Make use of existing symbols.** Symbols are available for computer-aided design programs. If you are working in an area for which symbols are needed (for example, electrical installation design), there are symbol libraries available. Rather than having to draw your own symbols, you can load them and insert them where you need them.

11 **Your computer can be used for video editing.** Professional video editing needs timecodes to synchronise sound and vision, but computers and ordinary video cameras can be used together for less sophisticated editing.

12 **Computers can be used for three-dimensional graphics.** This is a major growth area and special 3-D graphics cards can be installed in computers. These cards help the computer handle the complex calculations required.

19

Data communications

Computers can be linked together, allowing them to share and exchange information. By using the telephone network, it is possible for computers anywhere in the world to communicate. This is the basis for the Internet and networking. Modems, which are used for data communications via the telephone system, can send and receive faxes and are cheaper than fax machines.

1 **You probably have most of the hardware.** Most personal computers have a socket called a 'serial port' (or an RS232 port) which is often not used. This port can be used for data communications.

2 **You can experiment with two machines that are near each other.** Cables called null modem cables are available to connect two machines directly. They can be used reliably for distances of up to 50 feet (or 15 metres). A few different connectors are used, so make sure you buy the correct type.

3 **You may already have some data communications software.** Many operating systems include simple data communications facilities. They are also often included as part of many integrated packages.

4 **Use data communications to transfer large files between machines.** If you want to move data files between computers, you can often use floppy disks. If the files are too large to fit on one disk, this is more difficult. Data communications links can transfer any size of file, and are particularly useful for exchanging applications software between your own machine and machines at work (but keep an eye on copyright and licensing matters).

5   **Make the most of your laptop if you have one.** Transfer data files between a laptop and a desktop machine or between incompatible machines. You can carry a laptop around for mobile working, then transfer the data files to a desktop when you are back at your office. If you can save data in 'text only', or ASCII format, you can use data communications to transfer files between virtually any computers.

6   **There is free communications software available.** A program called KERMIT is available for virtually any computer. It is freeware and can be used to communicate between any machines for which it is available.

7   **Use a modem to communicate via the telephone system.** In order to use the telephone system, the data from your computer needs to be converted into a suitable form (and translated back again when you are receiving it). Modems do this. You will need one at each end.

8   **Experiment using an internal telephone system.** If your organisation has an internal telephone system, you can use it to link computers together via modems. There will be no telephone charges to pay.

9   **Think hard about whether to buy an internal or external modem.** Internal modems are fitted inside your machine. They are neater and usually slightly cheaper, but you will need to take your machine apart to fit one and it may be harder to set up correctly.

10 **Buy the fastest modem you can afford.** Prices are falling regularly. Faster modems take less time to handle data and so are cheaper to run, saving on telephone charges.

11 **Laptops can be linked to mobile telephones.** This is the ultimate in portable computing, but unfortunately it can only be done with special phones and is very expensive.

20

Networking

Networking can be considered as an extension of data communications. It enables larger numbers of systems to be linked together. Peripheral devices, such as printers and scanners, can be shared. Even more importantly, data files can be shared between users, helping with collaborative work. Running a large network is a job for a full-time specialist, but simple networks can be set up within an office relatively simply.

1   **You may already have the software.** Many operating systems include basic networking software.

2   **A few manufacturers include networking hardware.** If operating a simple network is a priority, investigate this before you purchase. Network cards are not very expensive, but you need one for each machine on your network, so this can add up to a considerable sum.

3   **Fitting network cards is not difficult.** Most personal computers will need to have internal cards installed to handle networking. Taking the computers apart to fit them is not difficult, but care is needed. If you are not confident, seek help rather than risk damaging your equipment.

4   **You will need cables to link the machines together.** These cables are not simple to make yourself, so you will probably need to buy them ready-made. You may also need terminators for the ends of cable runs.

5   **Put one person in charge of the network.** Someone needs to control the operation of the network. It might as well be you! Appoint and train a deputy so that others can cope if you are not there.

6 **Think about security.** Networks make data more widely available, so if there is need for protection of data, you will have to increase security when you install a network. Users can be issued with identities and passwords which they will need to use to access data. You can also use these to restrict data to certain users only.

7 **You may need network versions of software.** If there can be more than one user of data at the same time, special problems can arise. What happens if two people try to alter the same data at the same time? You may need special versions of software that can handle these problems.

8 **Don't forget about copyright.** If you are using software on a network, you may still need a copy for each machine. Check that your licence covers this.

9 **Networks can allow savings on software.** It is often possible to buy software for use by several machines operating as a network. This can be cheaper than buying individual copies for each machine.

10 **Maintenance tasks can be quicker on a network.** Tasks such as installing new software can be quicker on a network. If you have a computer used to store the programs used by the other machines (called a file server), you may need to install and configure it once for the whole network.

11 **Put diaries on your network.** Diary programs can enable people to have their schedule available to others via the network. It is then possible for others to see their schedules and arrange mutually convenient times for meetings. It is possible to provide control over who can make entries in other people's diaries.

12 **Printer switches can help a group of users to share a printer.** This is nowhere near as sophisticated as a network, but they are cheap and simple to operate. The simplest (and most reliable!) printer switches have a mechanical switch that the user needs to set so that the correct computer is connected to the printer. More sophisticated switches connect a computer to the printer automatically when it is needed.

21

Getting to know the Internet

The Internet is a global network of networks. It is accessed by millions of computers all over the world and is a vast data resource. It is also very heavily hyped and needs to be viewed a little cynically. Nobody is in charge of it and there is no control over the quality of the data available on it.

1   **Find out if your institution already has Internet access.** If there are any computer support personnel available to you, ask them about Internet access. It is possible that they have already negotiated a deal and the easiest option would be to use this. If you have a computer on a network, Internet access may be available through this.

2   **The equipment you need is modest.** You need a personal computer, which need not be state of the art. If you are connecting via the telephone network, you will also need a modem. This modem should be fast, to reduce your connection charges.

3   **Software may be free, or included in a deal.** Some Internet software companies allow non-commercial users free copies of their programs. If you pay for Internet access, you may be supplied with the appropriate software.

4   **You will need to use a 'service provider'.** These companies allow you (for a fee!) to access the Internet via their system. They vary in facilities and pricing structures, so investigate exactly what is on offer before signing up. Check how long the service provider has been operating.

5 **Is there a local telephone number for you to use?** In addition to paying the service provider, you will have to pay telephone connection charges. If there is a local access point, your bills will be lower than if you have to pay for long distance calls.

6 **How fast are the modems at the access point?** Even if your modem is fast, it can only operate as fast as the one at the other end of the telephone line. If theirs is slow, your telephone bills will be higher.

7 **Use it at cheap rates if possible.** Reduce your telephone bills by using it at off-peak times as much as you can. Investigate special deals where telephone companies give discounts for calls to selected numbers of your choice.

8 **Investigate newsgroups.** Newsgroups are set up on the Internet for use by people with common areas of interest. You can read discussions about a very wide range of topics and you can make contributions. If you can find (or start!) a newsgroup about your special area of interest, you can discuss it with colleagues from all over the world.

9 **You can send e-mail anywhere in the world.** If you know the Internet e-mail address of another user, you can send them mail for the price of a telephone call. If it is a local call, at cheap rates, this is very cheap, and very quick.

10 **Use it in the mornings.** A very large proportion of Internet use is in the USA. When the Californians are using it, response is very slow. In the mornings in the UK, much of America is asleep, so the system is much faster.

11 **On-line Information Services provide information as well as Internet access.** There are several competing services that provide information such as dictionaries, encyclopaedias, share prices, road information and much more. These are usually more expensive than Internet service providers, but they provide high-quality information.

Chapter 3   IT And Teaching And Learning

In this chapter, we move away for a while from hardware and software, and touch on humanware! It's all too easy to get preoccupied with systems and programs, and forget about people. In particular in this chapter, we want to share with you some ideas on ways of using IT to help students learn – and also to help you to teach.

We start with a reminder of how students learn most effectively, and link this to the use of IT. We next turn to some general suggestions about how you can get the most out of using IT in your classrooms. We then move up in scale to some considerations you may find useful if you wish to use IT in large group lectures (more eyes on you when things go wrong!).

Next, we propose some suggestions about how IT can be used in assessment. In many ways, assessment tends to be the weakest link in the teaching-learning-assessment chain, and computer-based forms of assessment can (when well designed) take away some of the burden of marking, and can also be demonstrably fair and reproducible. In addition, computer-based assessment (particularly in self-assessment environments) can be an excellent way of giving students a degree of individual feedback which may not otherwise be possible, particularly in the context of large groups.

There has been (and continues to be) a rapid proliferation in the range of computer-based learning materials available. More and more teachers are designing their own programs. More use is being made of commercially available packages. We therefore move on to give some suggestions about choosing and using such materials, followed by some tips for readers who may wish to proceed towards designing packages of their own.

Information technology can be used to support learning in every imaginable subject. If we were to try to include suggestions about each subject we would need to write another book! We've therefore chosen to address science teaching and music teaching in order to demonstrate the vast range of subjects in which IT can be useful. We have included a set of suggestions on other subjects to start you thinking about what could be done in the context of your own subject.

We next turn to student groupwork. Information technology can provide a valuable basis for student-student interaction, and help maximise the benefits of peer group learning. Particular topics that follow on naturally from student groupwork include the use of simulations, and the use of information technology for surveys.

We end the chapter with some ideas which may encourage you to use IT to help you set up and maintain student records, including assessment data.

We realise that this chapter can only skim the surface in the context of the many ways IT can be put to good use to support teaching and learning, but we hope that our suggestions are sufficient to trigger your imagination towards realising the potential of IT in your own subject context.

22

IT and how students learn

In the next set of suggestions, we look at way that you can try to help your students learn effectively, with IT. You may, of course, adopt any of these to learn about IT yourself!

1   **Most learning happens by doing.** Getting students to learn anything connected with IT is best tackled by making sure that they have plenty of opportunities to get their hands on the technology. Students don't learn much from hearing us talk about IT.

2   **Feedback is vitally important in learning.** Students need to find out how their learning-by-doing is going. Often they will get immediate feedback, seeing whether or not what they are trying to do is working. It is valuable for students to also get feedback from experienced people, who can often see at a glance what their problems are.

3   **It is important that students *want* to learn.** When they are already highly motivated, they will learn well from almost everything they try with IT. If, however, they need 'warming up' to make them more interested in what they are learning, it is important to try to find ways of showing them tangible benefits.

4   **Give students the chance to make sense of what they're learning.** It is important that they have the opportunity to digest new things that they've learned. It's all too easy for students to be swamped by so many new stimuli and experiences that they aren't able to get a real feel for the important basics of each skill they learn.

5   **Remind students how useful it is to explain what they've just learned to someone else.** This is often the best way to consolidate their learning. Putting something into words to explain it is one of the best ways of the explainers getting their own heads round it.

6   **Make full use of students teaching each other.** Someone who has just grasped a new idea is often more able to communicate it to someone else than is someone who has understood it for a long time. The latter person may have forgotten the actual experience of learning it for the first time.

7   **It's alright to make mistakes!** In any kind of learning, mistakes are a useful way towards getting things right. In most IT learning situations, learning from mistakes is particularly valuable. It is worth designing exercises so that students can see for themselves the consequences of all the most probable mistakes. If they've never made a particular mistake, they may have missed what they could have learned from it.

8   **Learn a little, and often.** Few things are learned efficiently at a single sitting. It is best to build in repetition and practice for students, so that they relearn several times the really important (or difficult) things, until they are firmly conditioned not to forget them any more.

9   **Help students to become more conscious of how they learn best.** For example, when students have mastered something, get them to spend some time working out (and explaining to each other) exactly what helped in their learning, and what the obstacles were. The more we can help students to take control of their own learning, the more self-sufficient they become in their approaches.

10 **Try to ensure that learning is fun.** When students are enjoying an exercise or task, the time slips by faster, and they're more likely to continue to work at it. Find out from students the things that they particularly enjoy, and try to build more of these things into their learning.

23

Using IT in the classroom

Students learn best when they're experimenting themselves with IT rather than just hearing about it. Classroom work where students get hands-on experience, with support from you, is an essential part of their learning experience. The following suggestions may help you – and your students – get best value from such sessions.

1   **Have good reasons for using IT.** Work out what the intended learning outcomes are, and how they depend on IT being used in the classroom. Tell your students what the purpose of using IT is on each occasion you use it.

2   **Don't depend on everything being there and working.** Whether you're going to use IT yourself to demonstrate something, or get your students using it to learn something, a lot depends on everything being in working order. Try to arrange that you will be able to keep the room free for at least half an hour before your session, and check everything yourself if you haven't got a member of technical staff who can do it for you.

3   **Make sure that the students can see when you demonstrate something.** If they all have networked computers, see if you can relay demonstrations to each workstation. Otherwise, check that you're only demonstrating to a small number of students at a time, and that they can see exactly what you do at each step.

4   **Put instructions and commands down clearly in handout materials.** It's easier for students to work through a numbered sequence of operations, with each instruction short and sharp. When students have problems it helps if they can tell you exactly which step is causing them difficulty.

5   **Build in feedback for students.** When they're going through an extended sequence of operations, identify stages where they can get positive affirmation that everything is correct up to the stage they have reached.

6   **Make handouts visual.** Build in from time to time pictures of what students' screens should look like at key stages. Programs for printing screen dumps are useful here, allowing you to cut and paste such images into your handout materials.

7   **Identify the stumbling points.** Even with the best-prepared handouts and materials, there are usually points where some students encounter problems you hadn't thought of. Keep a note of these problems, and adjust your instructions and handout materials to minimise the likelihood of them occurring on future occasions.

8   **Where possible, get students learning by doing, at their own pace.** This allows you to walk around acting as troubleshooter and helper. Make sure that your help is equally accessible to students in far parts of the room – don't just help those at the front! Have a system whereby students needing your help signal you so that you can treat them in order of them alerting you.

9   **Make sure that students have the chance to consolidate what they have done towards the end of each session.** It's only too easy for students to find themselves being rushed to close things down when the session is coming to an end, without them having the chance to make sense of exactly how far they have got, and what remains to be done on the next occasion.

10   **Wind up your sessions in good time.** If the room will be needed by a colleague shortly after your session is scheduled to finish, try to ensure that everything will be cleared up and ready in good time. In any case, students don't like sessions which overrun!

24

Using IT in presentations and lectures

People's worst nightmares regarding using IT often hinge around things going wrong when everyone is watching them. There is no way of guaranteeing that every lecture will be a polished performance, but there are ways of planning to limit any damage that adverse circumstances may inflict. We hope the following suggestions will shield you from your nightmares.

1 **Keep it simple!** Each presentation or lecture you do isn't meant to be a Royal Institution Christmas broadcast event (which takes weeks or months to plan and make perfect!). Decide what you really need to use in each presentation, and have good reasons for including it.

2 **Make sure that things are visible to students.** Check if a video projector or LCD panel for an overhead projector is available. If, for example, you're using computer-generated slides to illustrate your presentation, ensure that font sizes are sufficiently large to be able to be read clearly from the back of the room. Alternatively, you can use monitors spread around a suitable room.

3 **Get your setting-up done without an audience!** It's a lot harder to get IT equipment ready for action when all eyes are on you. Most of us are much more likely to get mixed up in our preparations if there are people watching us.

4 **Allow sufficient time.** Many people who use IT in lectures or presentations cram too much into the available time, leading to rushed performances. Remember that there will be things you want to explain further when alerted to do so by the expressions on the faces of your audience. You may also have questions to answer, so leave plenty of time in reserve.

5   **Capture your message in print.** Even when using spectacular demonstrations of the power of IT, your audience should have something to take away to remind them about what they saw. This is particularly important when you're using a lecture to demonstrate things that you want students to do for themselves later; lists of the steps you take in each sequence will help them.

6   **Keep your cool when things don't work.** It's useful to be a role model for students at such times. Explain each action you take to try to get things working again, so that in similar circumstances they get an idea of the approach to take.

7   **Be ready for disasters!** Now and then there will be circumstances where you have to abandon completely any intention to demonstrate IT in a lecture (for example, if there's a power cut). Always have something up your sleeve to keep the session going. Have one or two tasks which you can keep the class busy with for a while; this may at least give you the chance to sort out what's wrong with the technology.

8   **Keep your audience interested – use variety.** For example, if projecting computer-generated images onto a screen, don't get too set on a particular format or housestyle. Audiences tire easily, and get fed up with a series of images which look too similar.

9   **Use your presentation package to produce your notes.** These programs allow you to produce detailed notes in conjunction with your slides. This will help you keep track of when to change slides during your presentation.

10 **A 'screen splitter' could help you work with large groups.** These devices enable the picture from one monitor to be displayed on several more. They are relatively cheap and can be a great help in ensuring that everyone in a group can see properly.

25

IT assessment methods

One of the most demanding and stressful jobs of a teacher is to assess students (and keep records of the assessments). IT can play a major part in assessment, and good use of computer-managed assessment can free time for you to be better able to help your students learn.

1 **Phrase your questions really carefully.** In multiple choice questions, for example, it is important that picking the right (or best) option is not too dependent on being able to make sense of the question itself.

2 **Try out your questions extensively before using them for an assessment which counts.** Questions which look good aren't always good assessment devices. For example, there's little point using a question which everyone gets right (unless you're deliberately using one or two of these to build up students' confidence).

3 **Plan carefully exactly what you are intending to measure using IT methods.** Structured tests can measure breadth of knowledge, or just memory. Such tests are less easy to use if you're seeking to measure students' abilities to argue a case or explain the rationale of a situation.

4 **Don't use throwaway distractors.** In multiple-choice questions, each distractor (wrong answer) should represent an error which some learners will make. When it's hard to think of the last distractor, try giving the question in open-ended form to a class – unexpected wrong answers will often alert you to good distractors.

5 **Make full use of the feedback that IT assessment methods can give students.** There should be a feedback message you can give for each distractor as well as each right answer. Even when the assessment is summative, it is useful for students to get a print-out of feedback comments for each question, as well as their overall score. Working out all these feedback responses takes time, but it is well worth doing, especially when large numbers of students will benefit, or when the questions will be used over and over again in future assessments (for example, as elements of a multiple-choice question bank).

6 **Make feedback comments complete in themselves.** When students read the feedback, they probably won't have the original questions in sight (except in on-screen computer tests). It is important to remind them exactly *what* they got right or wrong.

7 **Consider using optical mark reading for tests.** When student numbers are too large for on-screen computer-managed testing, you can still make use of technology to save you having to mark multiple choice or structured tests longhand. It is important, however, to get to know the strengths and limitations of the equipment at your disposal, and to run plenty of trial tests which don't count, before using such systems for important summative assessments.

8 **Use the computer to help you analyse students' performance.** Programs are available for doing all sorts of analyses, including working out the facility values and discrimination indices of your questions (ie measuring which questions distinguish best between the good candidates and the weaker ones).

9 **Make use of computer-aided self-assessment.** The availability of computer assessments to students can be a useful incentive for them to test out for themselves how they are doing. In such assessments, the importance of giving students good feedback is paramount. The computer can be programmed to keep track of the performance of your questions as well as of your students, and can help you choose good questions to use in later summative assessments.

10 **Get students themselves designing IT assessments.** This can be a stimulating basis for a student assignment. You may well be able to adapt the results for your own assessment bank in due course.

26

Finding, choosing and using computer-based teaching materials

It is often said that there is no point reinventing wheels. This is not quite true of computer-based teaching materials however, as there is a lot of useful learning to be achieved in reinventing such materials. That said, there is not usually time to do this, so it is well worth finding out what is available already before you start designing teaching materials of your own.

1   **Keep a running check on teaching materials that are already available in your field.** New materials are being produced all the time and it's hard to keep up with what is available. Going to conferences with exhibitions is often a useful way of finding out who is doing what in the general areas you teach. Asking around and finding out who knows what is the quickest way of tracking down materials you might consider.

2   **Join, or build a network of colleagues in other institutions.** It saves a lot of time having a grapevine – and it's enjoyable too. Using e-mail to keep up regularly with colleagues elsewhere can be effective, quick, and cheap.

3   **Try out some packages in a field you know little about.** This in some ways is even better than trying out packages you may decide to purchase or adapt, as you'll be better able to feel what it is like to be learning from scratch from the packages, rather than being tempted to quibble with the way the content is handled.

4   **Don't confuse price and quality.** The *real* quality of a learning package is to do with how well students learn from it, and isn't necessarily connected to how much it costs to acquire the package.

5   **Don't be taken in by the gloss.** Gloss comes in many forms – stimulating-looking packaging, on-screen graphics, handouts and brochures, and so on. A package can *look* very good without *being* very good. Conversely, some packages that don't look particularly good may work well in practice – though you may need to think about improving their looks, as students can also confuse looks with quality.

6   **Check carefully the stated learning outcomes.** Check that what the package claims to teach matches what your students need to learn. Then check whether the package really lives up to its claims. Don't consider packages that are only marginally related to what your students need to learn. They may be fun, but they bring with them the risk that your students may fail to achieve your syllabus objectives.

7   **Ask for references.** When you're seriously considering purchasing a package, ask its producers or marketers for names and phone numbers you can consult regarding how well it was found to work. Reputable suppliers will be pleased to pass on this sort of information.

8   **Check up about site licences and so on.** Often it can be economical to purchase a package with rights to use it throughout your institution or department, and with arrangements that you can copy it onto all machines on the premises, and maybe even issue or loan copies to students to use on their own machines.

9   **Enquire about updates.** Most good packages are updated and improved quite frequently. Some producers and suppliers have arrangements where you can be informed automatically about improvements, and often you can arrange to receive new versions at a very modest cost.

10 **When you've got a new package at last – use it yourself first.** It's little use just watching other people use it. To be able to use a package in your teaching, you really have to have experienced exactly what your students will be experiencing. Beware of being a victim of the 'not invented here' syndrome; often a package may approach something in different ways than you would have done, but as long as students learn effectively from it, this should be no problem.

27

Designing computer-based teaching materials

Setting out to design a computer-based teaching package of your own is an ambitious target. However, if you've been teaching a topic until you're really familiar with how students learn it, you're in a good position to consider this option. If you are serious about this, it's worth finding out about 'authoring' packages which can guide you through the key stages.

1   **Start by clarifying the intended learning outcomes.** Avoid resorting to academic language when expressing these outcomes. For example, if tempted to write 'students will understand the Second Law of Thermodynamics', ask yourself instead 'what will students be able to *show* for this understanding when they develop it?' and write down evidence descriptors based on this.

2   **Express the learning outcomes in language students themselves can understand.** Build statements of intended learning outcomes in to the start of your computer-based learning package, but don't just leave them there. As students come to each new part, remind them of what they are supposed to become able to show for their learning.

3   **Next, build tasks around the intended learning outcomes.** Most learning happens in a learning-by-doing mode. Designing a computer-based teaching package is very much the business of putting together a sequence of things for learners to do.

4   **Don't tell students anything you can ask them!** There's nothing more boring in computer-based teaching packages than screen after screen of information. Not much is taken in then. Ask students rather than telling them. Some will know already. Those who don't yet know can find out from your feedback responses to the questions you ask.

5   **Write good feedback responses.** It is not usually enough just to give the right answer to a question as feedback. Students want – and need – to know what was right or wrong about the answers *they* gave or the options *they* picked. They want to know 'was I right? If not, why not?'. Choose your words carefully to make your feedback explanations as understandable as you can.

6   **Try out your questions and feedback responses with live students.** You can learn a lot just by watching students answering your questions and seeing the expressions on their faces as they read your feedback comments. You can learn even more from their questions and problems. Often, all you may need to do to improve a question and response is adjust the wording a little.

7   **Route your feedback.** In computer-based teaching packages, students who have got something wrong don't necessarily need a long-winded explanation if they can understand a simple one. Using levels of feedback helps here – for example a help menu or button where those students who wish can have access to a more detailed explanation of a point.

8   **Don't underestimate the time it takes to put together a computer-aided teaching package.** It gets a lot faster with experience, but even then it usually takes several versions before you have a package which works smoothly and well.

9   **Build in tests.** When developing a package, tests are to measure the effectiveness of your package rather than to assess your students. In any case, tests help students themselves to take stock of the things they have learned, and the things they haven't yet learned successfully.

10   **Find out what students think about it.** As well as monitoring the effectiveness of computer-based teaching packages by measuring students' performance, it is well worth asking them how they feel about various aspects of the package, including the tone, style, quality of feedback, how interesting it is, and so on. The computer can help with the processing of the data you collect from students.

11   **If you need to produce large numbers of copies of disks, consider a disk-copying machine.** These machines are stacked with disks and then automatically produce copies. You could use one to prepare notes or other teaching materials on disk to distribute to students. They are expensive, however, so try to borrow one!

28

IT in science teaching

It's not automatic that science students are highly competent at using computers. Students with a bent for IT often are attracted to computing courses rather than science ones, so not all computer-literate students are good at science. The following suggestions may help to equip science students with a greater degree of IT literacy, and also spare them some of the tedious side of practical science data handling.

1 **Find out how IT literate your students already are.** It is useful to design a questionnaire to find out quickly which programs, concepts and packages your students are already familiar with. Expect to find a wide spread of computer literacy, and be prepared to build on the lowest common denominator, but with fast-tracking for students who don't need to learn the basics.

2 **Use IT to save students spending hours number-crunching.** In many areas of science, students need to handle experimental data, and display it as graphs, from which computations are made. Much of this can be done using computers. It is more important that students become skilled in interpreting data than merely handling it numerically.

3 **Make sure students understand what computers are doing for them.** Despite above points, it is well worth getting students to do the number-crunching *once*. This not only helps them understand the sequence of operations that the computer is doing for them, but also helps them gain ideas about how to harness the potential of IT in other computations and data handling they encounter.

4 **Use IT in tutorials.** For example, it can be useful to use some tutorial time getting students to process typical data from experiments they have not yet started. This means that when they

come to the real thing, they have a better understanding of how their data should look, and can spot more easily whether anything is going wrong.

5 **Have computers and useful software available in laboratories.** It is worth encouraging students to start their writing-up of experimental data as soon as possible – and in a location where they can get help if needed. It is also a way of keeping a check on how collaboratively students are working.

6 **Operate a booking system for computers and software that are in heavy demand from students.** This can also be a way of avoiding the cases of students who fail because they did not submit work, claiming they 'could not get onto a machine', appealing against assessment decisions on such grounds.

7 **When possible, link dedicated computers to particular experiments.** This helps ensure that students spend their time and energies on aspects of their work that are more important than data processing, and also helps students to appreciate that this is what is done in research and development work.

8 **Consider setting up virtual experiments.** It can be just as effective to learn from a computer simulation of a real experiment, and to process and write up the data as if it had been real. With a little imagination, all sorts of real experimental variables and errors can be incorporated into such programs.

9 **Don't make students do it all the time!** Sometimes, when students have already done a fair amount of experimental work, it can be just as instructive to ask them to write a report about how they *would have* gone about setting up an experiment and analysing the data. The analysis part can require them to describe how they would have used IT to process their data. Such tasks help avoid laboratory log jams where student numbers are high, and can also be used under formal exam conditions.

10 **Remember to do the experiments yourself too!** The results you obtain can be used not only to check that everything is working, but also as data upon which to base assignment questions, tutorial exercises, model answers, and exam questions.

29

IT in music teaching

Computers are often associated with technology and may seem unsuitable for teaching music. In fact, there has been a close association between computers and music for many years. This is particularly true for music produced using electronic instruments, but computers have their place in conjunction with all kinds of music. Computer programs are available for teaching many aspects of music.

1 **Computers are good for producing scores.** Score-writing packages let you have complete control over how music looks when printed. They make it very easy to edit your work and allow transposition with a few mouse clicks.

2 **MIDI can be used to connect instruments to computers.** Most electronic instruments can use a Musical Instrument Digital Interface (MIDI) to connect to each other and to computers. This means that your computer can record what you play and play it back later. This is ideal for preparing musical examples in advance.

3 **Use MIDI to enter music into your score-writing package.** Your playing can be transcribed very quickly. This is a good way of showing how what is actually played will not be exactly what is written. Slight variations in timing caused by your interpretation of the music will be shown by rests added to the score. If you want to tidy your score up, it can be quantised to (for example) the nearest semi-quaver.

4 **Use a sequencer to set up complete performances.** Sequencing programs can record every nuance of a performance on a MIDI instrument. They also include facilities to help with editing files to produce exactly what is desired.

5   **Musical sequences can be very useful for practising.** The music to be practised, an accompaniment or parts played by other instruments can be recorded and played back at any speed. Students can play along on their instrument and increase the speed of the sequence as they gain confidence.

6   **Instruments other than keyboards can use MIDI.** There are guitars, saxophones, flutes, drums and other instruments that have MIDI interfaces added. Be careful, however, because sometimes a major change in playing technique may be needed.

7   **MIDI can control other equipment.** Apart from playing music, MIDI can control music effects processors, mixing desks, recording machines and other musical equipment.

8   **Computers can control entire performances.** Via MIDI, almost anything needed for a performance can be controlled. Lighting and other effects, such as smoke generators, can be programmed in advance from a computer.

9   **Computers and hard disks can be used for multi-track recording.** This provides digital sound recording combined with the power of the computer. There is instant access to any part of the recorded material and the computer can process the recordings in very sophisticated ways. For example, it is possible to change the tempo of recorded music without altering its pitch.

10 **MIDI files are small compared to recorded sounds.** If, for example, you wish to add several minutes of sound to a multimedia presentation, recorded sounds would take a lot of disk space. A MIDI file to play the same music would be tiny by comparison.

11 **Music scanning software can read sheet music.** The result is a file that can be edited using score-writing software. Warnings about copyright are particularly appropriate here.

30

IT in other subjects

A computer program has been written for almost every subject that could be taught. Not all these programs are good, of course. Search in education catalogues and journals. Sometimes a program is written for a specific need and is then made available as shareware because the potential market is very small.

1   **Food preparation.** There are programs to help understand dietary needs. Recipe programs will suggest what to cook with the ingredients that are available.

2   **Astronomy.** Your computer can act as a sophisticated observatory. Given the date, the time and your location, an accurate map of the sky is produced. You can zoom in on areas of interest and find out the name of stars and constellations. CD-ROM versions often include photographs taken by space observatories. Programs are also available which can control telescopes and point them at any heavenly body. The telescope can be made to track fast-moving bodies as they move across the sky.

3   **Electronics.** Circuits can be designed and tested by wiring up the components on the screen. Voltages and test signals can be applied and the results monitored on screen with digital voltmeters or oscilloscopes. Printed circuits can also be designed on screen.

4   **Mathematics.** There are programs for teaching maths at all levels. Specific topics such as probability can also benefit from the use of computers.

5   **Languages.** CD-ROMs of resources and programs useful for teaching languages exist. Dictionaries held on CD-ROM allow much more sophisticated searching than the alphabetical listings in paper dictionaries. There are even CD-ROMs for studying irregular verbs in a number of languages. Language translation programs may be more a source of amusement than being of practical value.

6   **English literature.** Study guides on CD-ROM are available for a number of works of literature.

7   **Multi-volume encyclopaedias are produced on CD-ROMs.** In the case of the biggest encyclopaedias, it is cheaper to buy a multimedia computer and the CD-ROM than it is to buy the printed version. When in use, the search facilities to help users find information are much better than using the paper equivalent.

8   **Study skills.** There are several computer-based study skills development packages, many of which allow learners to complete questionnaires which are analysed to give them feedback about their strengths and weaknesses.

9   **Business studies.** Several companies produce and market software to help people develop a wide range of skills involved in business and management. These include giving presentations, accounting, leadership, stress management, and conducting meetings.

10   **Keep abreast of what is becoming available.** It is worth getting onto the mailing lists of the companies that produce and market subject-related computer software. A good way of finding these companies is to go to conferences and exhibitions where such companies display their wares.

31

IT and groupwork

Students learn a lot from each other. Indeed, it can be argued that they learn more from each other than from teachers! One way of maximising the benefits of student peer-group learning is to harness its potential by setting work designed for collaboration. This is particularly appropriate in topics relating to use of computers and information technology. The following suggestions may help you develop student groupwork.

1   **Decide on the intended learning outcomes of groupwork.** Make sure that these outcomes are seen as core ones, and not just optional extras. Specify the outcomes such that the collaborative nature of the work is included in them, for example, by reserving some of the assessment for group processes as well as group achievement.

2   **Use groupwork to accommodate limited availability of resources.** Getting students to access computers and databases as a groupwork task helps to address the problems of providing access to such technology to large groups of students. One member of the group can have primary responsibility for the group's use of IT and other tasks can be allocated among the rest of the group.

3   **Timetable student groupwork flexibly.** Particularly with large groups, you will need to ensure that students have sufficient access to the equipment and software involved in the groupwork you plan for them. It is important to avoid appeals against unsuccessful assessment based on lack of access.

4   **Use groupwork to allow computer-literate students to teach others.** Choose group membership so that each group contains someone who is already good at using computers or databases. Legitimising students showing each other the ropes saves you doing a lot of explaining!

5   **Make use of groupwork as a means of allowing students to learn at their own pace.** It does not matter if some groups take longer than others, if the final result is that all groups achieve their targets.

6   **Brief groups carefully.** It is useful to prepare printed briefing notes, and issue them as handout material in a whole class session, so that you know that all groups have received the same information in the same way.

7   **Address the issue of contribution.** When students know that their individual contributions to groupwork are going to be taken into account, they try harder to ensure that they participate equally. One way of putting this onto their agenda is to have a diary of the progress of the groupwork as one component contributing to the assessment of the work.

8   **Research students' problems with groupwork.** Each IT group-work project is likely to have its own set of problems. The more you can find out about exactly what these are, the better you can plan to minimise them on future occasions.

9   **Have a 'help' mechanism.** Some groups will need more assistance from you than others. When students are working in groups at different times, you will not always be available to help. It is therefore useful to advertise times that you will set aside for students to seek help.

10   **Consider the possibility of advanced students helping less advanced ones.** For example, it is possible to implement student proctoring, where a second-year student is appointed to help a group of first years on a project. The advanced students learn a great deal by explaining things to the newer ones.

11   **IT can be used by groups to keep each other informed.** It is very easy for a group member to produce multiple copies of an interim report for distribution to the whole group.

12   **Data communications can be used by groups.** Group members could use electronic mail or computer conferencing for some of their interactions. This would mean that they would need to meet less often.

13   **Computer diaries help with scheduling.** If group members have their diaries available on a networked computer, mutually free times can be identified and arrangements made very easily.

14   **Computers can remind group members of scheduled activities.** It is frustrating for a group to be thwarted because a member forgets to carry out scheduled tasks. The computer can remind people of what they should be doing!

15   **Data can be shared over a network.** When a group of people are trying to work together on a project, there may be delays because data is not always available when it is needed. If the data is held on a computer on a network, it can be accessed by any authorised person at any time.

16   **Groupwork will encourage learning about IT and how it is used in the workplace.** A group of people working on a task that involves IT will interact rapidly to develop their IT skills. They will also develop an increased understanding of the benefits of IT. These are bonus learning outcomes!

17   **Word processors can keep track of who has done what.** When a document has multiple authors, it can be difficult to keep track of amendments and additions. Investigate the word processor's abilities to display text according to who has typed or altered it.

18   **Make sure one person is in charge of what is going on.** It is very confusing if there is more than one version of a document in circulation among a group. One person should be given the job of collecting and collating everybody's work and producing an up-to-date version. Older versions must then be taken out of circulation.

32

Using IT for simulations

Some of the most powerful uses of IT revolve around simulating real world situations and environments. Students are being prepared to work in the real world, so simulations can play important roles in their education and training.

1   **Use IT to spare students from doing boring, repetitive calculations.** For example, with suitable software, students can bring trial-and-error approaches to finding out how changing each variable, one at a time, affects an experiment in science or engineering. Students can get a better feel for a situation in this way than that they would have gained by using maths or science equations to calculate the optimum conditions directly.

2   **Use simulations to save students time.** While in many subjects, direct experimental or practical work is important, it often happens that students spend too much time doing it. It is sensible to strike an appropriate balance between work where students get hands-on experience using experimental equipment, and work where they investigate similar situations but using computer-generated simulation environments.

3   **Use simulations for consolidation.** For example, when students have already done some practical work, computer-based simulations can be used to extend the range of this work to include other choices of conditions or environments. When they already understand what's going on in the simulation, they are free to experiment quickly by trial and error.

4   **Use simulations where experimental equipment is expensive or limited in availability.** While it is valuable for students to experience using a range of equipment, computer simulations can provide a way of helping all students to interact with the principles of the equipment, even when they only have limited time using the real thing.

5   **Use simulations to prepare students for the real thing.** When students already have an understanding of an experimental set-up, they get more out of the time they spend using actual apparatus and equipment. Simulations can be used to help students plan how they will approach the real thing when they have the opportunity to do so.

6   **Get students to write up a simulated experiment as they would have done a real one.** Computer simulations can be a vehicle for developing students' report-writing skills, not only helping them gather data quickly, but also helping them design professional presentations of the results of their experiments (such as printouts of graphs, charts and statistical information).

7   **Make simulations fun!** It is possible to build in to computer simulations many of the features which make computer games enjoyable. Student culture tends to be oriented towards such games already, so it is worth capitalising on such aspects of simulations.

8   **Help students to capture what they learn from simulations.** A danger of simulations is that though students may have a strong learning experience while working with them, they can quickly forget that experience later. It is useful to have some sort of paper-based digest of the main learning points, which students can retain and revise from later.

9   **Keep your ears to the ground, to find more simulations.** New programs are being developed all the time. A good way of keeping up-to-date regarding what is available is to go regularly to conferences and exhibitions. Students themselves often know what's the latest thing!

10 **Make sure that students know the purpose of the simulation.** As always, it is very useful to be really clear about the intended learning outcomes. When students know what they're looking for, they're more likely to find it.

33

IT and surveys

Information technology can save a lot of the time and work involved in designing questionnaires and conducting surveys. You may be involved in such work yourself, or you may be helping students to do such work as part of their studies. In either case, the following suggestions may make life easier, and help the results of the surveys to be better based.

1 **Use your computer to produce high quality questionnaires.** People are more likely to take a survey seriously if the forms look professional, so make the most of your desktop publishing program. If you use a lot of questionnaires, look for a special program for designing them.

2 **Work out exactly what you want to gather information about!** Too many surveys and questionnaires are loose, and respondents only have so much patience. It is usually better to have well-considered answers to a few important questions than surface answers to a wide range of questions.

3 **Make sure the questions are clear.** A problem with many surveys is that different people read different things into the questions. It is best to test out separate variables in successive questions than to have one question covering too many interpretation possibilities.

4 **Try out draft questionnaires early.** Even with a well-designed survey, you will often learn more about the design of the questionnaire from the first dozen replies than you would have learned by studying the questionnaire itself for hours!

5   **Ask your pilot respondents 'are there any better questions that should have been asked?'.** Often you will find some of the replies to this question well worth considering for the next edition of your questionnaire.

6   **Try to avoid respondents having to enter long answers.** Though it is often useful to have one or two 'free range' open-ended questions on a questionnaire, it is not easy to analyse a large number of answers to such questions. It is often possible to cover the same ground as could be done with open ended questions by turning typical answers to the questions, for example, those gathered from pilot version trials, into options which future respondents can select as components of structured questions.

7   **The data could be put directly into the computer by those being surveyed.** If you design a database or spreadsheet well, you can let people input their answers to questions directly into the computer. Their answers can be restricted to only allow valid entries. This saves you entering the data later, but means that access is needed to your computer.

8   **Computers can read some documents.** Special readers can detect marks on pages (such as boxes that have been ticked) using an Optical Mark Reader. This can enable rapid data collection if a survey is very large. This is a specialist area and is only worth considering for very large surveys.

9   **Some databases can carry out qualitative analysis.** These databases are often free-form and allow unstructured text to be entered. They can then examine the text against predetermined criteria to produce a qualitative analysis.

10   **Make full use of your computer's statistical abilities.** It can produce totals, averages, maximum and minimum values and a range of more complex statistical evaluations. Check what you will need and make sure you collect the data in a suitable form for the analysis that you will need to carry out.

34

IT and student records

Your computer can help you with all the administration tasks related to your job. These can often be carried out using a spreadsheet or a database, and so are good for learning how to use these packages. Take care to keep your paper methods going until you are confident that the computer solution is working properly and be careful about backing up your data!

1   **Use a spreadsheet to keep records of marks.** It is easy to set up a simple spreadsheet to store the marks for a series of assessments. You can then use the facilities of the spreadsheet to sort the data (alphabetically by name or highest mark to lowest mark) and to produce averages and other useful data.

2   **Save each version of your records.** When a new set of marks or data are entered, it's worth saving the spreadsheet under a new filename. This is invaluable on those occasions where data may have been entered into the wrong place somewhere, and you can then backtrack successfully and make corrections much more easily.

3   **Use computer-based records to help you with one-to-one student encounters.** When you can dial up the individual records of any student at short notice, you can save yourself time when individual students come to see you, or in personal tutorial work.

4   **Produce charts to show performance and trends.** These charts can help summarise complex data into a simpler format. This can help you produce presentations or spot trends in the performance of your students.

5 **Allow students to see the screen!** When you're looking through student assessment data while working with individual students, it is important that they can see for themselves the data you have about them. This can also help them see how their own performance compares (for example) with class averages.

6 **Use a database to store full details of your students.** The search facilities can be used to produce reports such as finding everyone on your course who has Grade 3 or less in GCSE Maths who is not taking the optional maths support sessions.

7 **Use mail merging to help write letters.** Your word processor can send letters to only those who meet set criteria and can include correct details for each individual automatically. For example, you could search for all those who have achieved a certain mark and suggest that they should apply for a prize.

8 **Use printouts of student assessment records to encourage punctual submission of coursework.** If you post a printout on a noticeboard very quickly after the hand-in date, those students who were late in giving in their work will see no entry beside their names. This usually spurs them to be more punctual in future.

9 **Suggest that individual students keep their own spreadsheets of their assessment records.** Where students are using spreadsheets anyway, it can be good practice for them as designing something of their own, and it can also serve as a means of reminding them of their own progress, and working towards their own targets.

10 **Comply with the Data Protection Act.** If you are keeping records about individuals on a computer, you must register with the Data Protection Registrar and comply with the regulations. This is not difficult and you may find that your institution can provide you with help over this.

Chapter 4   More Bits And Pieces

Our final chapter is in a sense 'any other business', but also relates to a number of themes which should be borne in mind in the preceding chapters.

We start by taking a look at multimedia – a term which seems endemic in discussions about computer-based teaching and learning nowadays. We then focus in on one particular medium, print, with some suggestions about printers. We focus outwards next with some general ideas about maintenance of your hardware.

Our next two sections are about laptops: 'Computing on the move' and the more specific agenda of 'Writing on the move'. More and more people take their 'office' with them when they travel, and developments in hardware and software make it possible to continue to work on sophisticated packages under battery power (for as long as that lasts!).

We next take a look at some of the peripherals, such as monitors, keyboards, mice and speakers. We continue by extrapolating a bit further with a section called 'Space junk', which is intended for the wealthy and wise (computer-wise) rather than new starters to computing.

A separate set of suggestions on 'Computing and the law' follows next. The legal side of information technology continues to develop rapidly, but we provide some key points to check up on.

Next, we provide 20 tips on 'Security', which is about making sure that you don't lose your work. This leads naturally into 'Viruses', which are another way of losing your work!

We end the book by adding a bit more to the visual side of information technology, with suggestions about putting pictures into your work. Sometimes this can be done by using scanners, so we have added some suggestions on how to choose and use these. Our final set of suggestions leads outwards to your computer being the centre of your universe — just about anything you can think of is, or will very soon be, possible.

35

Multimedia

Multimedia computers have a CD-ROM drive, a sound card and loud speakers. These enable them to use detailed graphics, sound and moving pictures. Well-written multimedia software makes use of these facilities to provide excitingly presented materials. The main breakthrough is the CD-ROM, which allows large amounts of data to be stored and distributed cheaply. CD-ROM speeds are constantly increasing and new, even higher capacity models are under development.

1 **There are agreed standards for multimedia computers.** In order that software can be produced to run on most machines, these standards are used. Because multimedia requires powerful computers and computers are developing all the time, the standards are regularly updated. These standards are called MPC (Multimedia Personal Computer) standards.

2 **New machines should be built to the latest standard.** New software will be written with the latest standard in mind and will require a machine that conforms to the standard to run properly. MPC1 and MPC2 standards have already been developed. MPC3 should be watched out for.

3 **Multimedia can be added to existing computers.** You could buy a system without multimedia facilities and buy them later. You will need to be handy with a screwdriver to do this, but it isn't hard. You can either buy the components to suit your needs and budget or buy a complete multimedia kit in a box.

4 **Look at prices carefully.** It may be cheaper to buy a system with multimedia installed than to add it later. On the other hand, if you don't need it now, it could pay to wait as prices tend to fall rapidly. You may be able to save money by, for example, using speakers and an amplifier that you already have.

5 **You may need a special card for showing video on your computer.** Videos tend to be small, slow and jerky on many computers. Some videos use MPEG (Motion Picture Expert Group) compression to make data files smaller. These files need to be de-compressed before being viewed. Unless your computer is extremely fast, you will need an MPEG card in your machine to view them.

6 **Multimedia development is time-consuming and expensive.** All the sounds, pictures, text and movies need to be obtained in digital form before the work of linking it all together to form a cohesive structure is started. Recordable CD-ROM drives are expensive and reproduction of CD-ROMs for small runs is very expensive.

7 **A vast range of multimedia titles already exist.** Searching in catalogues may reveal something that will do the job you need.

8 **Having a multimedia system doesn't mean you have to use all the media at all times.** You can, for example, take a break from the computer and listen to a music CD with such systems, or listen while you write on the computer.

9 **Setting up your newly delivered multimedia system can seem a daunting task.** However, you're very unlikely to do anything irreversible. Reputable suppliers often offer hotline support, and this is very helpful. Someone who knows the system can talk you through most difficulties you may meet over the phone. Alternatively, don't underestimate the value of using a handy teenager − most of these seem to come programmed with skills which let them get the most complex systems working by trial and error! You will, however, have difficulty getting them off your system when you want to use it!

10 **Many students spend a lot of time playing with multimedia packages.** Games, for example, on CD-ROM are highly popular among students. This means that there is already a substantial basis of expertise among students regarding accessing and using multimedia programs, and it is worth using this expertise to further their learning.

11 **It enhances your own credibility with students.** Being able to speak the same language as computer-literate students is a worthwhile benefit for you, too!

36

Printing

Despite dreams of the paperless office, computer systems are incomplete without printers. It is important to choose the right printer to make sure that you can do exactly what you need without spending too much money. Before you choose, look below at which printers are best used for which purposes.

1   **Use a dot matrix printer for cheapness.** These printers are slow, low quality and noisy. They are, however, very cheap to buy and run. You can even re-ink ribbons to save more money. They can usually use fanfold paper (with tractor holes down the edges) which helps them keep aligned during long print runs.

2   **Daisywheel printers offer very good quality – if all you want to print is made of letters.** They are rather noisy and can only produce a limited range of fonts. Extra fonts can be produced by changing the type wheel. They cannot produce graphics. Because of these restrictions, they are not popular nowadays.

3   **Inkjet (or bubblejet) printers are fairly cheap and can offer good quality.** They are very quiet and can be cheap to run, especially if you refill the ink cartridges. They can produce a wide range of fonts and graphics.

4   **Laser printers are very high quality and can be fast.** They are also quiet and are becoming cheaper. Running costs can be high but some suppliers will recondition and refill toner cartridges, which will save money. However, look carefully at the balance you need between speed and quality – some laser printers are very slow!

5 **Think hard about whether you really need colour printing.** Don't forget that colour photocopying is very expensive, so colour handouts are not usually feasible. If you do need colour, an inkjet printer will be the best option. Colour dot matrix printers are poor quality and colour laser printers are extremely expensive to buy and run. Paper and other stationery can be bought pre-printed with colour borders or backgrounds if you want to have a colour 'corporate image' on your work. One reason you might want colour is if you want to produce colourful overhead transparencies to support major conference presentations, if you give such things!

6 **Colour inkjets should also have a black cartridge.** If a printer tries to produce black by mixing colours, the result is a muddy brown. The expensive colour cartridges are also used up rapidly. Some of these printers allow you to change between colour and black cartridges, but the best have both fitted and use the correct one automatically.

7 **Inkjet printer inks are often not waterproof.** This can be disastrous, so check yours and take appropriate measures. If you produce address labels, the ink may run in the rain!

8 **Inkjets are sensitive to the type of paper used.** With some papers, the ink bleeds into the paper, causing blurring. Experiment with different papers if you are disappointed with the results. Try to test a sample before buying reams of paper. You could also find that one side of the paper is better than the other. For the best results, special coated papers are available (at a price).

9 **You can print onto overhead projector transparencies.** Make sure you are using the correct kind of transparency material. If you use a normal transparency in a laser printer, it can melt inside the machine and severely damage it. Inkjet printer ink will not dry on ordinary transparencies, but it will on special ones. Try to test samples before you buy, as they are expensive.

10 **Use a bureau for really high quality work.** There are bureaux who will print computer files to your specification. They have expensive machines to produce high quality, but discuss the process with them thoroughly before you produce your work so that you can provide it in the correct format for them.

37

Maintenance

Your computer system doesn't need a great deal of care and attention, but a little will help it last longer and make it more pleasurable to use.

1   **Be careful about using water or solvents on the equipment.** Read the instructions and only use what is recommended. If in doubt, test your cleaning process on part of the system which is normally not in full view.

2   **Cleaning the screen will improve your view.** Buy some screen wipes and use them regularly. It will really help. They should also reduce the build up of static electricity on the screen.

3   **Clean your mouse regularly.** If your cursor moves in jerks, your mouse probably needs cleaning. Most mice can be cleaned by turning and removing a plate so that the ball can be taken out. Wipe the ball clean and gently remove any dirt from the rollers inside. Cotton buds can help with this. Using a mouse mat will help your mouse work smoothly and help keep it clean.

4   **Keyboards can be cleaned too.** This is a fiddly job, but you can use screen wipes to clean the key tops if they become disgustingly dirty and sticky. You may need moistened cotton buds to remove stubborn deposits. You can also turn it upside down and shake it to remove crumbs, paperclips and other debris. Keyboards can also be vacuumed gently.

5   **Desperate measures can be tried.** If, for example, you spill a cup of coffee in your keyboard and it won't work any more, you may have to buy a new one anyway. As a last resort, before spending money, try washing it out in a bowl of water with washing up liquid. Drain it and let it dry thoroughly before trying it. If it still doesn't work, you haven't lost anything. Do not try this on anything that plugs directly into the mains, such as the computer itself, monitors or printers. Better still, don't spill coffee in your keyboard!

6   **Floppy disk drives can be cleaned too.** If a drive becomes unreliable, it is worth trying to clean it with a special kit. Don't do this as a matter of routine, though, because it causes extra wear.

7   **Keep equipment covered.** Dust and general dirt will harm all equipment. It is worth buying or making covers, particularly for keyboards. Thin membrane covers can be bought for keyboards which allow them to be used with the cover fitted, giving protection to the keyboard all the time.

8   **Clean your printer, too.** After much use, printers can build up accumulations of dried ink and paper dust. Follow the manufacturer's instructions to keep them clean.

9   **Keep your computer in the correct conditions.** Heat, liquids and dust are bad for your computer. Make sure you follow the manufacturer's recommendations about the conditions your computer works in.

10 **Consider using a 'screen saver'.** If your computer is left switched on all day, every day, there is a risk that images could be permanently burnt into your screen. This is particularly likely if there is always a menu bar in the same position. Screen savers put a constantly moving picture on the screen after a few minutes of disuse, preventing this burning while showing that the computer is still switched on. When you press a key or move the mouse, the computer returns to normal operation. Make sure, however, that a screen saver does not constantly access your hard disk, or prevent any power-saving measures from operating.

38

Computing on the move

If you travel a lot, particularly by train or plane, you may want to be able to carry on working during your journeys. You could also take a computer with you so that you can give presentations or so that you can communicate using a modem.

1 **Laptop computers are expensive.** In order to justify the cost of a sophisticated laptop computer, you will need to use it a great deal. You may be able to compromise with a less sophisticated model for travelling, and a more powerful desktop computer for use at work.

2 **Laptop screens can be hard to work with.** You may find it tiring to look at the screen for long periods. In particular, it can be hard to see the cursor when it moves. This may be worse in poor light and you won't have control over lighting when travelling. Check out the screen and cursor aspects before buying. Programs are available to change the shape and size of the cursor, which may help.

3 **Battery life can be limited.** Laptop computers will need to be run on their own rechargeable batteries when there is no mains supply available. Check how long the computer will really run for (not what the manufacturer claims). You may need to budget for extra batteries as part of your purchase.

4 **Laptop computers can feel heavy.** Even a few pounds can be tiring if you have to carry it a long way. Remember you may also need to carry extra batteries and a mains supply as well as the computer.

5   **Check the keyboard carefully.** Laptop keyboards are small and usually incorporate some compromises to provide the same range that is available on a full-size keyboard. This may mean some alterations to your typing, which will need practice. Laptops don't always have a separate numeric keypad, so if you're used to using one for entering data for calculations, you may have to learn to be equally adept with the numbers on the qwerty keyboard.

6   **The mouse can be a problem.** When you are travelling, there is often nowhere to operate a mouse. Various solutions have been tried, such as trackballs and trackpads. Make sure you are happy with the alternative provided on any laptop you consider. Don't forget that it is more difficult to use trackballs on moving vehicles than when sitting at a stationary desk. You could use external devices, but this will increase the amount that you have to carry.

7   **Some laptops have 'docking stations'.** When you're not actually travelling, these enable you to use a full-size monitor, connect easily to a printer or network and use a full-size keyboard by putting your laptop into a module. This means you use the same computer, whether on the road or at work.

8   **Consider alternatives to full-powered laptops.** If your needs while travelling are simple, you could buy a cheap device that would let you, for example take notes. You could transfer these notes to a desktop computer when you are back at work and finish them using a word processor. Investigate the possibilities of 'palmtop' computers, 'message pads' and even the better electronic organisers. Some of these are very powerful and surprisingly small and light, and have long battery life.

9   **Be careful about battery charging.** Follow instructions on battery charging very carefully as incorrect use can shorten battery life considerably. In particular, don't charge a battery until it is completely flat to avoid the 'memory' effect that can reduce the amount of charge a battery can hold.

10 **Use a timer to avoid overcharging batteries.** When batteries are charged for too long, they can be damaged by overheating. It is easy to forget to turn the charger off, so use a cheap mains timer to turn off the power after the recommended time.

39

Writing on the move

The following tips are intended for people who do quite a lot of writing on the move, and are based on our own experience, learned by trial and error.

1   **Choose suitable writing tasks for your travels.** Writing on the move is usually best with jobs where it's alright to do a little at a time then return to it (like writing this book!).

2   **Write, but don't edit much.** While in motion on trains, for example, it is much easier just to type material in than it is to go backwards and forwards making amendments and corrections. Getting the cursor to exactly the bit you want to change is not too easy when the journey is a bit bumpy!

3   **Save the fiddly jobs for later.** Editing, spellchecking, adjusting the layout, and so on, are best done when you're on terra firma. Another reason for this is that such operations run your battery down faster than just typing in new material.

4   **Choose jobs where you don't need lots of reference materials to hand.** There's not usually much room when writing on trains or planes to spread books and papers out around you. It is normally possible to get a single document somewhere suitable, but not a pile of papers and books.

5   **Choose your company!** People tend to be fascinated by the sight of people working on laptops, and this may put you off. It is better, for example, to sit in the airline-style double-seats on busy trains than at a table designed for four people. Some trains have one or two single seats which are ideal even on very busy trains – if you can find them!

6   **Have a multimedia journey!** It is worth having your Walkman or Discman with you — if you're already carrying a laptop, spare battery and mains lead, it won't make much difference to the weight. Listening to something of your choice while you write saves you being put off by children being normal children, football fans, or even being distracted by those fascinating conversations one only hears on trains!

7   **Call in for a pint and a Watt!** On long journeys, you may not be able to find somewhere to give your battery a top-up, but you can usually find a power point in a hotel lounge or even the station buffet. It's best to be a valid consumer when you're consuming just a little bit of electricity too!

8   **Keep saving to floppy disk as well as the hard disk.** When travelling, you never know when you may suddenly be interrupted. For example, when told to change to a train that isn't broken down! In the rush of gathering up your bits and pieces, it is only too easy to forget to save that last bit you've written.

9   **Carry a three-way mains adaptor.** Your hotel destination will probably have rooms where there is a shelf or other hindrance which stops you plugging in your mains connector directly into the power. With a three-way adaptor, there is much more chance you can apply some suitable geometry, and get charging again. It may also mean you can both write *and* boil the kettle for that coffee you need!

10 **Consider having a backpack.** This can be a better way of carrying relatively heavy laptops and accessories around, and means you have hands left for other luggage, train doors, and to hang on when lurching to a stop!

40

Monitors, keyboards, mice and speakers

When we choose computers, we are usually concerned with issues such as the type and speed of the processor and the amount of memory it has. In practice, you will probably scarcely notice if these components are not state of the art. Much more immediate concerns are the devices that we interact directly with – the monitor, keyboard, mouse and speakers. These issues are all subjective, so try to make sure that you exercise choice.

1   **The right monitor is very important.** Blurred, distorted or flickering pictures can soon cause eyestrain and make the whole IT experience an unpleasant one. Try to see the monitor in action before you buy. If this is not feasible, reviews of computer systems should comment on the quality of the monitor. It is particularly important that you buy the correct monitor first time, as they are expensive.

2   **Make sure the monitor is the right size.** Generally speaking, the larger the monitor the better. Unfortunately, larger monitors are also more expensive; 14-inch monitors are acceptable, but 15-inches are better. For design work, a 17-inch monitor is considered necessary, but if you want to work on double page layouts, a 21-inch monitor will be needed. A large, good quality monitor could cost more than the rest of your computer system!

3   **Check what area is actually usable.** The sizes given refer to a measurement across the diagonal of the monitor's picture tube. The usable area will be smaller – in some cases considerably so.

4   **Avoid interlaced monitors.** Some cheaper monitors use a technique known as interlacing to produce pictures containing a lot of detail (high resolution). The result is a screen that flickers uncomfortably.

5   **Make sure that your computer can support a larger display.** The monitor is controlled by special graphics circuitry. This can be part of the computer's main board or a separate card plugged in inside the computer. If you decide to buy a larger monitor, ask your supplier about this.

6   **Some monitors can be used in landscape or portrait mode.** These monitors are mounted on a tilting base so that you can turn them on their side. The picture is then redrawn so that it is the correct way up. This can be very useful for page layout and for spreadsheets.

7   **Keyboards vary enormously.** At first glance they all look much the same, but there are variations in the layout, in how far the keys travel and how strong the springs are. There are keyboards that make claims about ergonomic design. If possible, try them out to make sure you are happy before buying. If you are really unhappy with your keyboard, they are relatively cheap to replace. Nearly all keyboards are grey.

8   **Mice are not all the same.** If you use a mouse all day long, your wrists can develop surprising amounts of tension. Using a mouse of the correct shape can help reduce these problems. There are also ergonomic mice which claim to be designed specially to minimise problems. Some manufacturers even produce left-handed versions. Note that if your computer uses a two-buttoned mouse, you can usually adjust your operating system to reverse the button positions if you are left-handed.

9   **Cordless mice are available.** This means that you haven't got that annoying bit of wire coming out of the front of your mouse. If you have the money and don't object to mice without tails, this could be a good idea!

10 **Consider alternatives to the mouse.** Trackballs, trackpads, graphics tablets, lightpens and other devices are available if you really can't stand mice. However, there are people who really can't stand any of these, so find out what you prefer.

11   **Are your ears being offended?** Many speaker systems supplied with computers are very poor quality. You may consider this to be of low importance if you are not working with sound, but if you have a CD-ROM drive, you can have music while you work. It is much nicer if it is nice-sounding music! If you have an old hi-fi, you could use it with your computer. Keep the speakers away from your monitor and floppy disks to avoid damage caused by the magnetic fields from the speakers.

41

Space junk

This is a term for all those gadgets that sound as though they belong in science fiction stories, but are actually here now. They may not be common and are, in many cases, in an early stage of development. If you need to be among the first to use them, or if they fulfil your particular needs, find out more about them before you get left behind.

1   **Computers can speak.** Yes, they do sound a bit robotic, and they often have American accents, but even relatively humble computers can speak quite well. Programs can read any text out loud to you. This can be a great benefit to people with impaired vision. Others have tape recorded the computer reading articles they want to read and played the tapes in the car.

2   **You can speak to your computer.** You don't even need to be mad! Programs that let you control your computer by speaking to it are quite common and are sometimes included with sound cards. This is of little benefit to many users, but people with disabilities preventing normal computer use could benefit from this. These programs are limited to recognising commands that can be given from menus. Much more expensive programs exist which can type what is spoken to them. With practice they can be very effective.

3   **Computers can control machines.** You don't need sophisticated robot arms to do this. Several companies that make construction sets for children also make interfaces that enable the computer to control motors and other devices. They also supply sensors for heat, light and other factors to enable quite complex systems to be computer-controlled.

4   **Digital cameras can send pictures to your computer.** If you need to put images onto your computer very quickly, you can use one of these devices. They are available at a range of prices, and the quality of the images they produce is related to this. Check how many pictures they can take between battery charges. If you need to take large numbers of pictures, make sure they can store the images on floppy disks before you download them to the computer. Make sure you have plenty of disks with you when you are out with the camera.

5   **Your computer can display television pictures.** Cards can be fitted inside computers to enable them to act as televisions. The pictures can even be captured on the hard disk for later use.

6   **Your computer can also be a radio.** Complete radios on cards can be added to computers and the computer can be programmed to switch them on and off on the correct channel at predetermined times.

7   **Use your computer for video conferencing.** By adding small, cheap cameras and microphones to computer systems, video conferencing can be carried out over a network. Tutorials need never be the same again!

8   **Operate your computer with a remote control.** If you are using your computer to give a presentation, you can use a hand-held remote control to operate it. This means that you needn't give presentations from the front of the room.

9   **Scan photographic slides into your computer.** Slide projectors are old hat, so investigate one of these scanners. You can then use them in a trendy multimedia presentation without going out to take all the pictures again with a digital camera!

10   **Data watches can link up to computers.** These watches can exchange data with computers by being held up to the screen. They can store all kinds of data, such as telephone numbers, but with the benefit of using your computer's facilities to enter (and back up) the data. They can also be programmed to sound alarms and display appropriate reminders when the alarms go off.

11   **Machines can now scan, print and photocopy – all in colour.**
These machines are very expensive at present, but if your needs
include a fair amount of colour photocopying, the price will seem
more reasonable.

12   **Your computer can tell you where you are.** Navigational devices
called Global Positioning Systems are available and are reducing in
price. These use satellites to calculate their position to within a few
metres. Some of these systems can be linked to computers to
provide sophisticated control over navigation.

42

Computing and the law

It is possible for computer users to unwittingly break various laws. Penalties can be severe, so make sure that you are not operating illegally. The laws relating to computing are constantly changing as technical developments raise new issues, so try to keep up-to-date.

1   **Most computer programs are copyright.** In order to use them legally, you need to pay. If you use a copy of a program that has been pirated, you are committing an offence. If several people need to use the same program on several computers, a copy must be bought for each computer. Some software companies will operate a licensing scheme to reduce the costs of multiple copies. Do not give copies of programs to other people.

2   **Shareware programs must be registered.** You are allowed to try these programs before you buy them and you can often give them to others to try. If you find them useful and want to continue to use them, you need to pay a registration fee. Details of how to register should be distributed with the programs.

3   **Pictures, movies, sounds and other files may be copyright.** If you want to use someone else's work, make sure you know what the copyright situation is and seek permission to use it if necessary. Copyright-free pictures and other materials can be obtained and used.

4   **Copyright problems only usually happen when you come to publish or sell something you've done.** You are unlikely to end up in court until your criminal activities are put into the public domain! However, it is still worth being careful.

5   **Copyright your own work.** Work you do on your own computer at home, in your own time, is your intellectual property. Look after it. It can help to print © and your name on printouts, but in fact, you still own the copyright without doing this.

6   **Check whether your organisation has claims on your work.** If you are using hardware or software belonging to your organisation, or time paid for by your organisation, or even your organisation's electricity, the organisation may have claims over copyright of your work. Find out what the attitude is regarding intellectual property.

7   **If you keep personal data, you need to register under the Data Protection Act.** In order to protect the public, there are restrictions on what personal data can be kept on computers and how it can be used. Contact the Data Protection Registrar for details of the restrictions and to obtain a registration form.

8   **You can be personally liable under the Data Protection Act.** Even if you are working for an organisation and you are keeping personal data for the benefit of the organisation, you could be prosecuted as an individual. Make sure the necessary procedures have been followed to protect yourself.

9   **Be aware of health and safety regulations.** Make sure that any computer you buy or use conforms to these regulations. Also make sure that working conditions and practices are satisfactory. Examples of these include the levels of radiation emitted from the monitor and the lengths of time spent working at the computer. These regulations are for your protection, so don't ignore them.

10 **Check your insurance.** This doesn't just mean check that equipment you own is properly insured and that materials you borrow with permission from your organisation are covered. It is also worth finding out how you stand regarding professional indemnity matters; working for an organisation often affords you such cover. Your trade union may also be a source of advice on such cover.

43

Security

As you make more use of your computer, you will gather increasing amounts of data. In time, this data may become more valuable than your computer system. If you were to lose the data, it might not be possible to re-create it. Even if it was possible, it could be very time-consuming. In some cases, the data could be confidential and in need of protection from prying eyes.

1   **One day, your computer will fail.** All machines will break down. What you don't know is when this will happen. It is vital that you have some strategy in place to avoid losing your data. In an emergency, you could always use your data on a different machine.

2   **Back up important data.** It is usually most convenient to save your data on the hard disk of the computer that you normally use. If you don't want to risk having to re-create the data, save it somewhere else as well.

3   **Think about how much data you can afford to lose.** If you back your data up once a day, you could lose a whole day's work. If this sounds like too much to risk, back up more frequently.

4   **At very least, use a simple backup strategy.** The simplest method is to save your work to a floppy disk as well as the hard disk a few times a day. For extra security, you could use two floppies as well as the hard disk. Have a number on the end of your file name (such as number 1 to start with) and use Save As when you save your work. Each time you save, increase the number by one. If you do this, you prevent the computer writing over older versions of the file and you will have a series of files you could go back to. You might decide, at the end of the day, that you preferred the version you produced at lunch time. You will, of course, fill your disks more rapidly, but you

can delete old versions when you are sure they are no longer wanted.

5 **Store your backups somewhere safe.** If there was a fire, or a theft, you could lose your computer and your backups. Keep a backup somewhere away from your computer. Take it home, or swap backup disks with a colleague for mutual safety.

6 **Consider a more systematic backup strategy.** The simple strategy above will probably be satisfactory for many people, but there are still risks. What if a disaster strikes while both copies are together? What if a computer error or a virus damages both copies of the data? One strategy is to keep several 'generations' of important files. Only the oldest is brought to the computer at any time, to be overwritten with the latest copy. These techniques are sometimes called 'grandfather, father, son'.

7 **Are your system and program files safe?** You should be able to re-install your operating system and all your programs in the event of a major failure. This will be time-consuming and annoying. If you have customised your system by changing large numbers of settings, it could take a very long time to redo all this. If you do a complete system backup, you could restore the whole system if you need to.

8 **Consider a special backup device.** Floppy disks are fine for backing up small amounts of data but are very time-consuming and expensive to use for larger backups. There is a variety of devices designed for larger backups, including tape streamers, exchangeable hard disk units and digital audio tape drives. If you want to do large backups regularly, investigate these.

9 **Use appropriate backup software.** Most operating systems include software for backing up. Other software is available for the job. It may be faster, use less storage space for the backups, allow a wider range of options or help with automating the process.

10 **Test your backup devices and strategies.** It would be very upsetting to back your system up regularly only to find that you couldn't restore it when a problem arose. Make sure that it works before disaster strikes by testing the system's ability to restore from the backup device.

11 **Use passwords to protect your data.** Many computer systems allow you to use passwords to prevent unauthorised use. Check up on this and, if you use it, keep your password safe.

12 **Sometimes you can password-protect data files.** When you save your work, there may be an option to password protect it. On some systems you can lock files so that they can't be accidentally overwritten.

13 **Don't use passwords that can be guessed easily.** Avoid your names, or those of your family, friends and pets. Don't use 'password' or 'testing'.

14 **Don't forget your passwords.** This is embarrassing and counter-productive. You should, however, avoid writing them down and leaving them near your computer!

15 **Be careful about deleted files.** When files are deleted from a disk, they are still there! What happens is that the space that they used is marked as available for reuse and the file names are removed from the directory. Someone with a moderate level of computer knowledge could undelete files and gain access to their contents. Software is available to destroy deleted files properly.

16 **Power supply problems can destroy data.** It is fairly obvious that a power failure can delete work that you have just done. They may also corrupt complete files and disks. Less noticeable problems, such as power surges or spikes, can cause similar problems. Try to avoid plugging your computer into a supply near heavy machines or other sources of sudden power demand.

17 **Power conditioning devices are available.** These vary from simple special plugs that smooth the worst of the surges from the supply to complete backup power systems that switch in to power your computer in the event of a major power supply problem. You can even buy software which, in conjunction with a backup power supply, will automatically save your work and close the system down safely. When the power is restored, your work will be returned to its previous state.

18   **Protect your computer against theft.** Even if it is insured, you will suffer great inconvenience if it is stolen. You could also lose your data with it, if you don't have a good backup strategy. Lock the room where it is kept and consider using alarms. Make sure it can't be seen from outside the building. Security devices are available to fix it to an immovable object with cables or to lock it inside a steel case.

19   **The ultimate backup is a printout.** Despite the desire expressed elsewhere for a paperless office, one way of protecting your work from system failures or viruses is to print it out and store the paper copy somewhere safe. In the event of disaster, your thoughts are not lost. They can be retyped or scanned into the repaired or replaced computer.

20   **Exchangeable hard disks can improve security.** These devices enable you to remove one hard disk and insert another. You can use them to back up your main hard disk to store in safe places for security purposes. You could also use different disks for different projects.

21   **Don't rule out a safety deposit box!** If you're working on something that your whole career may depend on, it is not unreasonable, for peace of mind, to store both an interim disk copy and a paper copy somewhere as safe as possible.

44

Viruses

Computer viruses are actually programs written by malicious people. Their effects vary, from putting nuisance messages on the screen to destroying all the data on a disk. They are quite common, but it is usually simple to avoid problems.

1 **Be careful about disks you have been given.** If someone has a virus on their machine, it could be passed on to your machine via a floppy disk you are given.

2 **Viruses can be spread over networks.** Network managers should be aware of this and should take appropriate measures to prevent this happening. If you use a small network, there may not be an experienced manager to look after this.

3 **Beware of games disks that are handed round.** Your children (or those of your colleagues) may use virus-infected games on a computer at home. The virus can spread to work data disks and then infect other machines. Discourage use of games disks (unless they are the original disks) on machines you have contact with.

4 **Viruses can be downloaded from bulletin boards or the Internet.** When you use a modem to download programs, there is a risk that they could be infected. Responsible service providers will carry out virus checks on the software that they make available.

5 **Anti-virus software will help.** There are several companies selling software to help with viruses. These programs will, with varying success rates, detect viruses and warn you of their presence. In some cases, the virus can be removed successfully, but sometimes the infected files will have to be destroyed.

6   **Make sure that your anti-virus software is up-to-date.** New viruses are developed all the time, so anti-virus software is constantly changed to keep up. The virus writers are always one move ahead, but you are unlikely to be exposed to the latest viruses.

7   **Careful strategies are needed to deal with virus outbreaks.** If you have a severe virus problem, with many affected disks, the problem can be eradicated if a systematic approach is used. Follow the instructions with your anti-virus software to the letter. At very least, you will need a 'clean' machine with a guaranteed infection-free operating system that can be used to clean infected disks.

8   **Viruses can be present in 'macros'.** Until recently, viruses were only written to affect program files or the boot sector of a disk. Data files could not contain viruses. This has changed because many computer applications (such as word processors and spreadsheets) incorporate programming languages to produce automatic routines, or macros. Viruses that can destroy data have been written using these languages. Anti-virus programs may not detect these. To avoid problems, don't run strange macros and turn off any options for 'start-up' macros to be run automatically.

9   **If your computer suddenly starts to behave strangely, don't panic.** You could have a virus, but it is possible something else is the cause. Either way, the best approach is to keep calm and think hard or seek help before going any further.

10   **Keep it in proportion.** The majority of computer users will never come across a real virus.

45

Putting pictures on your computer

One of the benefits of using computers for producing documents and presentations is the ease of incorporating pictures. This is only possible, however, if you have the picture on a disk in the first place. There are various ways of doing this.

1 **Clip art can be very useful.** Disks and CD-ROMs of simple drawings are available for incorporation into your documents. Try to build up a collection and have some idea of where to find them.

2 **Collections of photographs are available on CD-ROM.** These are often high quality, but the files are large and may be expensive.

3 **Can you find an existing picture to edit?** You may have an illustration that is not quite what you want, but if you can load it into a suitable package, you may be able to adjust it to suit your needs.

4 **Can you draw it yourself on the computer?** Even if you lack artistic ability, you may be able to produce simple, stylised drawings to get the point across. The extensive Undo facilities in drawing packages are a great boon.

5 **Use a scanner to put an illustration onto the computer.** If you have something suitable on paper, or if you can take a photograph, a good scanner will do the job. Scanners can be expensive and experience in using them will help produce good results, so see if you can find someone to help.

6 **Photographs can be processed onto CD-ROMs.** Some of the very large photographic processors can take a film from an ordinary camera and produce the images onto CD-ROM ready for entry into a computer.

7 **Digital cameras are on the market.** If you plan to use a very large number of photographic illustrations, these are a possibility. Good ones are very expensive, however, and may be hard to justify. Because they do not use films, running costs are very low.

8 **Could some students produce artwork for you?** Investigate the possibility of having art students produce illustrations for you, perhaps as part of a project.

9 **Mice are not very good for drawing.** Try writing your signature on the screen using a mouse if you need proof. A better option is to use a graphics tablet. This is an electronic pad that you use in conjunction with a special pen in order to draw on the computer. The better ones have a pressure sensitive pen that gives you control over effects such as line density, depending on how hard you press. Some pens even have a 'rubber' on the other end.

10 **Animations can be produced by computer.** These could be used to illustrate processes such as the operation of a chemical plant or machine. You can even produce complete movies, but don't expect to compete with Hollywood immediately!

11 **Be careful about copyright.** If you are using someone else's artwork, check what the copyright situation is before having it reproduced.

46

Scanners

Scanners can be very useful alternatives to use for inputting data that you already have in printed form. Several different types are available and you need to consider your needs carefully before buying. In particular, the resolution of the scanner (the number of dots per inch it can recognise) is very important.

1   **Hand-held scanners are cheap, but only low resolution.** These devices look a bit like overgrown mice. You hold them in your hand and move them over the area you want to scan. They are fine for small jobs, such as scanning in a simple drawing or small amounts of text.

2   **Practise with your hand-held scanner.** Results from these scanners are often disappointing at first. Don't give up, though, because if you practise, you will be able to move it more steadily and straighter.

3   **Hand-held scanners are very versatile.** Because you move them by hand, they can be used to scan small pieces of paper, photographs or book pages. You can even scan items like pieces of wood or fabrics with them.

4   **Sheet-fed scanners are mid-price and mid-resolution.** These machines vary in shape, but look a bit like a small printer. If you feed a sheet of paper into it, it will be scanned into the computer. They can produce results good enough for many users, but they are restricted to scanning flat pieces of paper.

5   **Some sheet-fed scanners have feeder trays.** These trays can hold about ten sheets of paper and automatically feed them into the machine for scanning. This could be a major time saver if you need to scan long documents.

6 **Flat-bed scanners are more expensive, but can be very high resolution.** If you need to produce high quality images, you will need a scanner that holds the paper flat while it works. If you only occasionally need this level of quality, try to use someone else's scanner.

7 **Check how good the OCR (optical character recognition) software is.** Most scanners come with OCR software that reads printed text. This enables you to load the text into your word processor for editing or other work. This can be a great time saver, but some OCR software introduces so many errors that it is not worth using. The best OCR software is very good if the original document is printed clearly.

8 **Most OCR software can't cope with ornate characters.** If a document has been printed in a very fancy font, the software will make a lot of errors. You could utilise this if you want to make your work harder for others to scan. It also, of course, makes it harder to read!

9 **Do you really need colour scanning?** Unless you are planning to scan colour photographs or pictures, a black and white scanner may be a better deal. You could buy a better quality machine for the money.

10 **Be careful about copyright and plagiarism.** Scanning documents can be very easy, but think carefully before reproducing anything you scan in case you are breaching copyright.

47

Using your computer as a complete communications centre

By putting together a few of the technologies currently available, your computer could play a vital role in handling all your communications. It can even work when you are not there, taking messages and faxes for you.

1   **A fax modem can send and receive faxes as well as working as a modem.** Many modems include fax facilities. The software often allows you to print documents to the fax modem instead of to the printer. You need to provide the telephone number (or choose it from an address book on your computer) and the computer does the rest. If any faxes come in, your computer will notify you of their arrival and you can read them later.

2   **A scanner can be used in conjunction with the fax modem.** If you want to send a document that is not on your computer, scan it into a suitable program and fax it.

3   **Good quality printing is possible when you receive faxes on a computer.** You can use your inkjet or laser printer to produce a high quality printout that will not fade.

4   **OCR (optical character recognition) can be used on faxes you receive.** This will enable you to load a document that you have received by fax into your word processor for further work. This, of course, depends upon the fax you receive being good quality.

5 **Voice fax modems can handle telephone calls, too.** These devices can use your computer to provide a sophisticated telephone answering service as well as the features discussed above. They will automatically detect whether an incoming call is a voice call, a fax or data. They can provide telephone 'mail boxes' for a number of users so that a telephone caller can leave a message for the appropriate person by pressing a key on their telephone when prompted.

6 **Some communications devices will work when the computer is not switched on.** Some voice fax modems can store messages in their own memory, or switch the printer on to print out a fax.

7 **There are ways of staying turned on!** Power saving facilities make it feasible to leave many computers permanently switched on. This means that they can wait until an incoming message wakes them up while consuming very little power.

8 **Having everything to hand saves time.** A system which includes fax, phone, printer and computer saves journeys from one instrument to another. Fax machines serve as photocopiers for small jobs, and an immediate copy is better than having to wait in a queue at a photocopier!

9 **Incoming printed items can be scanned into the computer.** This is a step towards the paperless office. Instead of cluttering up your space with paper, all the documents could be on the computer, along with all the electronic documents you receive. However, you will need a large hard disk with a good filing system and a systematic backup procedure!

10 **Computers can be operated remotely.** If you have a mobile computer with a modem, you can access your desktop computer via its modem and interrogate it to check incoming messages. You could even find documents on its hard disk when you are not in the office.

Conclusions

In this book, we have covered a lot of ground and addressed a wide range of possibilities regarding the use of computers and information technology in teaching, learning, and assessment. However, we are the first to admit that there are all sorts of things we haven't even started to address in this book. Some of the missing dimensions we are aware of, but we are only too keen to be alerted to others that we would never have thought of.

We cordially invite readers of this book to write to us (care of Kogan Page) with suggestions regarding important bits we have missed. We are particularly interested to hear from readers who would like to compose some suggestions in the same format as we have done, on topics we haven't addressed yet. We will be only too pleased to incorporate these (with due acknowledgement and permission) in the next edition of the book.

Equally, we will be pleased to find out where we've got it wrong! Please do not hesitate to give us constructive critical feedback. We learn the same way as you, and your students — having a go, getting things right, getting things wrong, and finding out what people think about it.

If there is one conclusion that we hope you will come to from using this book, it is that virtually anything can be done with IT. Once you have decided what you need to do, it is only a matter of finding out how to go about doing it. As with many things, when we know the questions, we are well on the way to some answers. We hope our book will provide you with questions as well as with some of the answers. Over to you — and good luck with your computing!

Further Reading

In line with the style of this book, here are a few useful tips you should bear in mind when choosing a book to help you get further with your computer.

1   **Make sure that the book is written for the computer system you are using**. For example, there are books on PageMaker for the Macintosh and for the PC. If you buy the wrong one, some of its contents might not apply to your system.

2   **Make sure that the book is written for the correct version of the software you want to learn about**. For example, if you are using Word 6, don't be tempted buy a reduced-price book on Word 5 as the product has changed since the older book was written.

3   **Browse through the book to make sure it is at the correct level for you**. You should look for a book that starts with introductory material that you might already be familiar with, but it must contain material that will advance your knowledge.

4   **Test the book's index**. Go to the bookshop armed with a question that you need an answer to. Does the book's index help you to find the answer easily?

5   **Don't be put off by 'patronising' books**. There are several series of books (such as the 'Idiots' or the 'Dummies' books) that you may find rather insulting in tone. If they contain the material you need, they can still be very useful.

6   **Some books include disks or CD-ROMs**. This can make the books seem very expensive. If the extra material on the disk or CD-ROM is good, it is good value for money, but sometimes this material is very poor quality. It will be difficult to evaluate it, but check the book to see what the content is.

7   **If you like a book, look for others in the same series**. You will be used to the style and layout, so learning will be easier.

Other books on computing

The titles below represent a very small sample of the range of computing books available. If the topic you want isn't covered here, a good bookshop will probably have several books you could choose from.

Aitken, P (1994) *The Complete Idiot's Guide to 123 for Windows*, QUE, Indianapolis, USA
This book is on a current version of Lotus 123, one of the very first spreadsheet programs. This series of books covers a wide range of topics in a very idiosyncratic style. You may find it patronising, but the material is good.

Byrne, J (1995) *Easy Access for Windows 95* QUE, Indianapolis, USA
This is a good, clear introduction to Access, the database part of the Microsoft Office suite. There are several other computing titles in this series.

Cassel, P (1995) *Teach Yourself Access 95*, SAMS, Indianapolis, USA
This is another book on Access, from another series of computing titles.

Kennedy, J (1995) *UK Comms Information Superhighway*, BSB, St Albans, UK
This book gives a very clear introduction to many aspects of data communications, including the Internet.

Kent, P (1994) *Complete Idiot's Guide to the Internet*, QUE, Indianapolis, USA
This is a book from another series, which gives a simple introduction to the Internet. Again, its tone is a little insulting.

Levitus, B (1994) *Macintosh System 7.5 for Dummies*, IDG Books, Foster City, California, USA
The 'Dummies' series gives clear help in using a range of computer packages. This one is helpful for people who are learning to use Macintosh computers.

McKelvy, M (1995) *Using Visual Basic 4*, QUE, Indianapolis, USA
Visual Basic is a package for writing programs, so if you want to learn how to do it, this book could help. There are other computing books in this series too.

Mueller, S (1995) *Upgrading and Repairing PCs*, QUE, Indianapolis, USA
There is a great deal of information here if you have an old PC that you want to keep going a bit longer.

Nadler, B (1994) *Computing for Cheapskates* Ziff-Davis Press, Emeryville, California, USA
Need we say more? There are plenty of hints here on saving money!

Nelson, S (1995) *Field Guide to PCs*, Microsoft Press, Washington DC, USA
If you want to know more about your PC and how it works, this is a useful book.

Other books on teaching and learning from the same stable

Race, P and Brown, S (1993) *500 Tips for Tutors*, Kogan Page, London
A wide-ranging set of tips for lecturers of the Kogan Page '500 Tips' covering most aspects of teaching and learning.

Brown, S and Race, P (1994) *Assess Your Own Teaching Quality*, Kogan Page, London
A series of checklists with which you can self-evaluate the ways that you teach (and the things you don't yet do!).

Brown, S, McDowell, L and Race, P (1995) *500 Tips for Research Students* Kogan Page, London
If you are a research student using *500 Computing Tips* to help you get into computers, the above may also help you make sure that your research doesn't get put into second place due to the temptations to play with computers too much!

Race, P and Smith, B (1995) *500 Tips for Trainers*, Kogan Page, London
This book is aimed at people who plan and run training workshops. If you're likely to use IT in such workshops, this book should complement the present volume well.

Brown, S, Race, P and Smith B (1996) *500 Tips on Assessment*, Kogan Page, London
If assessment is a major part of your work, computers may help you keep records and deliver feedback quickly and efficiently. However, it is even more important to make sure that you are assessing the right things in the best ways, and that assessment contributes positively to your students' learning. That is the primary purpose of the above book.

Glossary

ASCII This stands for 'American Standard Code for Information Interchange'. Each character (such as numbers, letters of the alphabet and punctuation marks) is represented by a number. Because it is a widely used standard, computer systems can often understand each other by using ASCII codes. *See page 51.*

backup Computers can break down, so it is a good idea to keep security copies of important data. This is called a backup copy. *See page 110.*

boot This is a term for starting up a computer. Normally the hard disk of a computer contains all the instructions for a computer to boot up correctly and this happens automatically when it is switched on. A floppy disk can also be used to boot up a computer if the hard disk is not working properly. If your computer crashes, it may be necessary to 're-boot' it by pressing a reset button, or by turning it off then on again.

bulletin board This is a service provided on a computer which can be accessed using your modem and data communications software. They can be used to download software onto your computer and for other activities. Some charge a membership fee and others gain revenue from premium rate phone charges. *See page 13.*

CD-ROM These disks store vast amounts of computer data. They look exactly the same as audio CDs and use the same technology. They are normally 'read only', which means that the contents are permanently fixed. *See page 90.*

Clip Art This is the name given to small pieces of artwork that can be incorporated into computer files. These can be bought on CD-ROMs or disks. *See page 116.*

computer conferencing This enables a group of computer users to contribute to a discussion of a topic. As with e-mail, participants can be anywhere in the world if the Internet is being used.

configure Computers and software can be configured to change the way they work. For example, the contents of the menu bar of a word processor could be changed.

daisywheel printer   These printers use a wheel with characters on it to print, using a ribbon. They are high quality, but noisy and they are restricted to only printing the characters on the wheel. *See page 92.*

database   Database programs are used to process textual and numeric data, such as personnel information or spare parts inventories. They store data and allow it to be edited easily but, more importantly, have powerful facilities for retrieving and processing data. They are very versatile and modern ones can handle pictures and sound as well. *See page 40.*

desktop publishing   This refers to using to using a program on a computer to produce high-quality printed documents. Desktop publishing programs usually allow better control of the finished result than word processors. *See page 44.*

desktop computer   These are the normal big, heavy, mains operated computers that sit on our desks staring at us.

dot matrix printer   These printers use little pins struck against a ribbon to produce marks on paper. They are very cheap, but the printing is poor quality and they are noisy. *See page 92.*

download   This describes the process of a computer receiving data from another computer. *See page 13.*

drive   A device into which a disk or tape is placed for use.

e-mail   This enables a computer user to send a message to another computer user. E-mail is often available to users of a network. The Internet enables e-mail to be sent to any other Internet user in the world, usually for the price of a local telephone call. *See page 55.*

field name   When using a database, each piece of data must have a name, so that it can be filed away and retrieved successfully. Examples of field names from a personnel database might be 'Surname', 'Date of Birth' and 'Department'. *See page 40.*

field type   In a database, it is important to define what kind of data will be stored in each field. For example, much data can be stored in a 'text' field, but dates should be stored in a 'date' field if they will be needed for calculations. *See page 40.*

file name   When data is stored on a disk, it must have a file name so that it can be located and loaded later on. Computer systems have rules about the structure of file names, so make sure you are aware of them.

floppy disk This is a device used for storage of small quantities of programs and data. They can be taken out of their drive and so are useful for carrying data around or for small-scale backups. They are much slower in operation than hard disks. *See page 110.*

font Fonts are the typefaces used on computer screens and printers to change the appearance of documents. *See page 13.*

formatted disk When floppy disks are sold, they are usually unformatted. This means that they are completely blank, and the computer cannot store data on them until they are formatted. The formatting process puts a pattern on the disk that enables it to store and retrieve information. Formatting a used disk erases all the information on the disk.

hard disk This is a device used for storage of large quantities of programs and data. It is normally fitted inside a computer but external hard disks are also available. Some hard disks are also exchangeable, so that the disk can be changed while the drive remains in the computer. Generally speaking, hard disks should be as large and fast as possible.

import Programs can often use data produced in another program. In order to do this, the data is imported. If you try to import data, you may be asked questions about what program was used to produce it. *See page 44.*

inkjet printer These printers squirt ink onto the paper to form letters and other shapes. They are quite good quality and are fairly cheap. *See page 92.*

Internet This is a global network of computers. Literally millions of computers have access to it. Anybody with the correct resources can publish on the Internet and there is no control over the quality of the information provided. Many people's ideas about the Internet are based on the World Wide Web, which is a part of the Internet which uses an easy graphic interface. *See page 54.*

landscape Printers normally use the paper in 'portrait' mode, so that the page is taller than it is wide. Landscape mode turns the printout through 90 degrees, so that the paper is used the other way round. *See page 37.*

laptop computer Laptops are portable computers run from batteries and are small and light enough to carry around easily and use on your lap. *See page 96.*

laser printer   These printers use similar technology to photocopiers to produce high quality printouts. They are relatively expensive to buy and run. *See page 92.*

memory   This is the storage space available in the computer for it to store and run programs and data. Some memory cannot have its contents changed and is called 'read only memory' (ROM). The most important memory to check on is the memory that can be written to as well as read. This is called 'random access memory' (RAM).

menu bar   Most modern programs have a menu bar on the screen which is used to access commands. These commands control the operation of the computer. The commands are often selected with a mouse.

MIDI   'Musical instrument digital interface' (MIDI) is a standard way of connecting up keyboards and other electronic musical instruments. It can also be used by computers and other equipment, such as mixing desks and lighting controllers. *See page 74.*

modem   A device which allows computers to speak to each other using the telephone network. A modem is needed for each individual computer that needs to use the telephone. Many modems can receive and send faxes and some can also handle voice calls. *See page 50.*

monitor   This is the box with your computer that looks like a television set. They are not all the same! *See page 100.*

mouse   This is a small device that is moved by hand around a flat surface. As it is moved, so a cursor or arrow moves around on the computer screen. The mouse will have buttons to press to select operations. Mice are commonly used to control the operation of modern computers. *See page 101.*

multimedia   Multimedia means the use of computers to handle high-quality sound and graphics, as well as the normal text output. Computers need a CD-ROM drive, a sound card and loudspeakers to handle multimedia. *See page 90.*

operating system   Computers need programs to make them work, even when you aren't using a program to do anything. These programs are the operating system. They carry out tasks such as putting the display on the monitor, printing your work and saving and loading files. When you are using a program, such as a word processor, the operating system is working in the background.

optical mark reading   This refers to a technology which can detect the presence and position of marks on paper. As an example, it can be used to check which boxes have been ticked on a questionnaire. *See page 65.*

peripheral   Peripherals are all the extra devices that can be attached to your computer, such as printers, scanners and modems.

processor   This is the 'brain' of your computer. It is the component inside that makes the machine work and processes the data that is entered into it. Processors and computers are constantly becoming faster and more sophisticated, so sometimes older processors can be very slow or cannot use modern software.

scanner   This is a device that can read printed pages into the computer. They can read pictures and can often also convert text into a word processor document, ready for editing. *See page 118.*

screen dump   A screen dump records exactly what is on the screen at a given time. This can include the menu and tool bars and the cursor, so they can be very useful for producing instructions on computer use. There are several good screen capture programs available for producing screen dumps. *See page 61.*

screen saver   If the same image is left on the screen of a computer monitor for very long periods, it can become burnt into the monitor. The image appears as a 'ghost' all the time. Screen savers create a moving image on the screen when the computer has not been used for a few minutes. This prevents the burning taking place. *See page 18.*

site licence   If you have a large number of computers, it can be very expensive to buy the software for each one. Some software companies will provide a site licence which allows the software to be used on a large number of computers without having a copy for each. *See page 67.*

software   This another name for the programs that a computer needs to make it work. They are sets of instructions that have been written for the computer and tell it what to do and how to do it. *See page 22.*

spreadsheet   These are programs used to carry out operations on numbers which are arranged in rows and columns. They were originally developed for accounting purposes, but have a very wide range of uses. They can usually generate high-quality charts and graphs from the data that is produced. *See page 36.*

toner   This is a very fine powder used in laser printers to make marks on the page (the 'ink'). It is usually provided in cartridges that are put into the printer. *See page 92.*

toolbar   Most modern programs have a toolbar on the screen. It usually contains little pictures (called 'icons') which enable an operation to be carried out by clicking them with a mouse. It is usually possible to configure a toolbar to show commands which you use frequently.

virus   A virus is a small, self-replicating program that can be spread from one computer to another by infected disks, without the user realising. Viruses are designed to be malicious and can destroy computer data. *See page 114.*

word processor   The most common use of computers is word processing. It enables the user to produce very high quality documents, set out exactly as required. It is easy to edit documents before printing and to reuse parts of old documents. *See page 30.*

Index

In this index, we have not tried to list references to terms or words like 'information technology' or 'computer', which occur throughout the book. We have tried to make the index a useful way of tracking down the aspects of the book that are most relevant, or most interesting, to you.